THE WI BOOK OF
JAMS
and Other Preserves

PAT HESKETH

EBURY
PRESS

ACKNOWLEDGEMENTS

Illustrated by Vanessa Luff
Edited by Sue Jacquemier and Rosemary Wadey
Designed by Clare Clements
Cover photography by James Jackson
The publishers would like to thank the dozens of WI
members who tested the recipes in this book.
Some of the recipes on pages 14–16, 18–19, 22, 24, 26,
30, 36–40, 47–8, 50–1, 56–8, 63, 68–70, 72, 76, 80,
82–3, 85, 87, and 90–1 are based on recipes from *Bulletin
21 – Home Preservation of Fruit and Vegetables* (HMSO
1971) with the kind permission of the Controller of Her
Majesty's Stationery Office. The author wishes also to
acknowledge the advice given by the staff of the Home
Preservation section of the Long Ashton Research
Station, Bristol.

Published by Ebury Press
National Magazine House
72 Broadwick Street
London W1V 2BP

ISBN 0 85223 307 8

First impression 1984

© Copyright 1984 by WI Books Ltd.

Filmset by
D. P. Media Limited, Hitchin, Hertfordshire

Reproduced, printed and bound in Great Britain by
Hazell Watson & Viney Limited,
Member of the BPCC Group,
Aylesbury, Bucks

CONTENTS

INTRODUCTION

Foods have been preserved by many methods over the centuries, but in particular by drying, salting and freezing. Traditionally this has enabled housewives to provide a varied menu throughout the year. Modern growing methods and air freight have meant that most fruits and vegetables are always available in the supermarkets, but when locally grown fruits and vegetables are at their peak, they are relatively cheap to purchase, and great personal satisfaction can be achieved from the making of preserves, and from seeing a larder containing a good selection of home-produced preserves.

Three types of preserves are relatively easy and cheap to make and are eaten by most families: jams, marmalades and, to a lesser extent, some vinegar preserves such as chutneys. Using fruits and vegetables in season means they are at their best and their least expensive, and will bring welcome variety to meals at other times of the year.

To ensure that fruits and vegetables keep well when preserved, it is necessary to understand a little about enzyme action and about the control of spoilage organisms – yeasts, moulds and bacteria.

The action of enzymes brings about the natural ripening of fruits and also, given time, their decay. So it is necessary to stop enzyme action when fruits are ripe. This can be done by heat, as when making jams and bottling fruit, and also by low temperatures, as in the freezing of foods.

Yeasts, moulds and bacteria are micro-organisms which can be killed by high temperatures and also have their growth inhibited by high concentrations of sugar and high acid content. Methods of making preserves take these principles into account.

Jams, jellies and marmalades should have a sufficiently high sugar content to prevent fermentation, but they must also, after making, be covered in a manner which prevents the re-entry of airborne micro-organisms (see page 11).

Vinegar preserves should have a sufficiently high

acid content to prevent the action of micro-organisms, and they should also be covered in a manner that prevents the vinegar from evaporating (see page 65).

The type of vinegar to use is stated in the introduction to chapter 5. If in doubt, use malt vinegar unless it is a very pale coloured preserve or pickle, when a white, distilled vinegar is preferable.

Equipment
Preserves need very little special equipment and can be made quite satisfactorily with the equipment found in most kitchens. Here is a check-list:

preserving pan and/or	scales
large saucepan	measuring jug
mixing bowl	measuring spoons
small basin	large wooden spoons
plates	(one preferably a
colander	preserving spoon)
sieve (nylon)	tablespoon
small vegetable knife	vegetable parer
large chopping knife	mincer
chopping board	juice extractor

Further equipment which may be useful:

juicer	slow cooker
liquidiser/	microwave oven
food processor	pressure cooker

Preserves in the microwave oven
Microwave ovens are particularly useful for making small batches of preserves. Jams, marmalades and chutneys can all be cooked in a microwave oven. They require less time and less attention than when cooked conventionally, but the container used for cooking must be about three times as large as the amount of ingredients being used. This will allow for the preserve to 'boil up' without spilling. It is recommended that the advice in the instruction book for each microwave oven be followed, but many of

the recipes in this book can be made successfully using a microwave oven, providing it is remembered that only small quantities may be cooked at a time.

Measurements
All spoon measures are level unless otherwise stated.

3 tsp = 1 tbsp
8 tbsp = ¼ pint = 5 fl oz = 150 ml

All eggs used are size 2 or 3 unless otherwise stated.

Use either the metric measures or the imperial in the recipes; do not mix them. They are not always equivalent to one another, because they have been tested and balanced separately.

All can sizes are approximate.

All weights referred to in lists of ingredients for fruit, vegetables, etc. are unprepared weights unless stated otherwise.

Presentation of preserves for showing
When entering a competition or show, it is necessary to read the schedule carefully so that the rules and instructions are fully understood.

It may help competitors to know that although only one mark out of twenty is given for the appearance of the container – that is, the cover, cleanliness of the jar and the label – if the cover is not suitable for the preserve and will not keep it in good condition, the judge may not judge the preserve at all.

The container must be suitable for the preserve and it must have the appropriate cover (see pages 11, 12, 65, 66 and 89 for further details). The jar should be well filled, and the glass can be polished with methylated spirits to remove fingerprints. For carrying to the show, place the jar in a polythene bag and wrap it in either newspaper or corrugated card and pack it in a box.

The label must be straight and should be parallel

to the bottom of the jar and placed as low as possible without wrinkling. The label should state: type of fruit, e.g. raspberry; type of preserve, e.g. jam; date of making, e.g. 3rd July 1984. If frozen fruit has been used, this should be stated, and also the date of making, e.g.:

Raspberry Jam
(frozen fruit)
10th January 1984

For bottled fruit the label should state the strength of the syrup or the usage to which the fruit may be put, e.g.:

Bottled Gooseberries		*Bottled Gooseberries*
(light syrup)	or	*(for pies)*
30th June 1984		*30th June 1984*

The label on chutneys should state whether they are mild or hot.

The colour should be good, and appropriate to the fruit the preserve was made from. In jams, jellies and marmalades the colour should be bright, even and sparkling. A dullness and slight darkening indicates overboiling of the preserve after the sugar was added. In chutneys, although the colour will be dark-ish, it should be bright, not muddy-looking.

The jar should be full – a low quantity in jams means that the cover is not able to do its job properly and that moulds may develop. A low quantity in vinegar may indicate shrinkage which is caused by evaporation of the vinegar due to an incorrect cover.

The consistency of jams should show a good gel, and if whole fruits are present, as with black-currants, or peel shreds as in marmalade, these should be soft. Check that they are before adding the sugar. In chutneys, if there is 'free' vinegar floating on top of the preserves, this indicates that the chut-ney was insufficiently cooked before potting.

The flavour should be characteristic of the fruit, not spoilt by the use of inferior quality fruit, nor by overboiling or burning on the base of the pan.

JAMS AND CONSERVES

In this chapter are some of the more traditional jam recipes using unusual fruits, and also exciting combinations of ingredients such as rhubarb with rose petals or angelica. If you like preserves with whole fruit in them, you will find here recipes for conserves, but remember that these will not set as well as jam does.

A good jam should: keep well; be clear and bright; be characteristic in colour; be well set, but not too stiff; have a distinct fruity flavour.

Jam is a mixture of fruit and sugar cooked together to form a gel. To obtain a good gel (set), acid, pectin and sugar should be present in the correct proportions. Fruits vary in their acid content and the amount of fruit used when making jam varies according to whether or not it is rich in pectin. Extra acid is often added to fruit to help release the pectin present. If frozen fruit is used, increase the amount of fruit in the recipe by 10%.

Good pectin content

Black and Redcurrants	Gooseberries
Cooking Apples	some Plums
Crab Apples	Quince
Damsons	

Medium pectin content

Early Blackberries	Loganberries
Fresh Apricots	Raspberries
Greengages	

Poor pectin content

Late Blackberries	Medlars
Cherries	Pears
Elderberries	Rhubarb
Marrow	Strawberries

Pectin Test

A test for *pectin* should be carried out after the initial cooking of the fruit with water.

1. Take 5 ml (1 tsp) juice, place it in a small glass. Cool.

2. Add 15 ml (3 tsp) methylated spirits.

3. Shake gently together.

If a well formed jelly-like clot is apparent, this shows a good pectin content.

If several small clots appear, this shows a medium pectin content.

If no clot appears, then no pectin is present.

If, after further cooking, still no recognisable clot appears, the addition of extra pectin will be necessary. This may be either juice from pectin-rich fruits, or commercial pectin. Use 50–100 ml per 450 g (2–4 fl oz per 1 lb) of fruit.

| Very little or no pectin content | Medium pectin content | Good pectin content |

Acid helps to give a bright colour and prevent crystallization. It must be added at the beginning of cooking to fruits low in acid and to any vegetable jam, in the following proportions:

To 1.8 kg (4 lb) fruit:

30 ml (2 tbsp) lemon juice (1 average lemon) or

5 ml (½ level tsp) citric acid or tartaric acid or

150 ml (¼ pint) redcurrant or gooseberry juice

Sugar. Granulated or preserving sugar may be used, but it must be thoroughly dissolved before the jam is brought to the boil. Many recipes are based on 60% sugar content, therefore if 2.7 kg (6 lb) sugar is used, a 4.5 kg (10 lb) yield could be expected.

Fruit should be dry, clean and fresh, and preferably slightly underripe.

Stages in jam-making

1. Initial cooking of fruit either on its own (e.g. strawberries) or with water. Fruit should *simmer* gently to break down the cell walls to release the pectin.
2. Carrying out the pectin test. A good result means that the cooking time with the sugar will not be prolonged and therefore the finished jam will have a good colour.
3. Addition of sugar, off the heat, stirring to ensure that it is completely dissolved.
4. Returning pan to the heat, bringing to the boil, and boiling rapidly until setting point is reached.
5. Putting into clean jars and covering immediately with either a wax circle or a pliable plastic top or a metal twist top. The jars should be filled to within 3 mm (⅛ inch) of the rim. A cover should be placed on each jar as it is filled.

The cellophane dust-covers used in conjunction with wax circles may be dampened on the upperside and placed over the jar when either hot or cold, but never when warm.

Tests for setting point

Saucer test (also known as plate, or wrinkle test). Have a plate cooling in the refrigerator. Place 5 ml (1 small tsp) jam on the plate and return to the refrigerator to cool for 1 minute. If the surface wrinkles as the finger is pushed through the jam, the jam has reached setting point. *It is important to keep the jam pan away from the heat during the test otherwise the jam may go beyond setting point.*

Flake test. Dip the spoon into the boiling jam.

Holding the spoon above the pan, twist it horizontally to cool the jam on the surface. Allow the jam to drop from the surface. If it has reached setting point the jam will run together and form a flake on the edge of the spoon before breaking off cleanly.

Temperature test. Place a sugar thermometer into the jam. Boil the jam until it reaches a temperature of 105°C (220°F).

Labelling
Clean the jars and label with details of contents and date of making (see page 7).

Storage
All jams are best stored in cool, dry, dark, well ventilated places. Storage is a problem in centrally heated homes. Therefore jars with metal twist tops are recommended, because when properly used these form an airtight seal.

Conserves
A conserve is very similar to a jam in its making but the result is different in that the set is much softer and some fruits remain whole in a thick syrup.

Sugar thermometer
and preserving pan

APPLE AND PINEAPPLE JAM

Makes about 6.5 kg (11 lb)

3 kg (6 lb) cooking apples
1.25 litres (2 pints) unsweetened
  pineapple juice
juice of 2 lemons
450-g (16-oz) can crushed pineapple
3 kg (6 lb) sugar

Peel, core and slice the apples. Place in a preserving pan with the pineapple juice and lemon juice. Simmer gently until the fruit is soft. Test for pectin. Remove from the heat.

Add the sugar and stir until dissolved. Add the drained crushed pineapple and return to the heat. Bring to the boil, and boil rapidly until setting point is reached. Pour into warmed jars, cover and label.

SEEDLESS BLACKBERRY AND APPLE JAM

Makes about 2.5 kg (5 lb)

2 kg (4 lb) sour green apples
juice of 1 orange
juice of 1 lemon
300 ml (½ pint) water
3 kg (6 lb) blackberries
sugar

Peel, core and slice the apples. Place in a preserving pan with the fruit juices and water. Simmer until tender. Add the blackberries, and simmer again until quite tender, stirring frequently.

Rub the mixture through a hair or nylon sieve and return to a clean preserving pan. To each litre of pulp add 750 g sugar or to each pint of pulp add 1 lb sugar. Stir until the sugar is dissolved. Return the pan to the heat, bring to the boil, and boil rapidly until setting point is reached. Pour into warmed jars, cover and label.

MARROW AND PINEAPPLE JAM

Makes about 3 kg (5½ lb)

2 kg (4 lb) prepared marrow
1.5 kg (3 lb) sugar
450-g (16-oz) can pineapple pieces

Peel the marrow, remove seeds and cut into small neat dice. Place in a bowl and sprinkle with the sugar. Leave overnight.

Next day, transfer to a preserving pan, add the pineapple pieces, chopping roughly if rather large and the juice. Bring to the boil, and boil until clear (about 1 hour). Pour into warmed jars, cover and label.

RASPBERRY JAM

Makes about 5 kg (10 lb)

3 kg (6 lb) raspberries
3 kg (6 lb) sugar

Place the fruit in a preserving pan and cook slowly to extract some of the juices, then simmer gently until the fruit is tender. Remove from the heat. Add the sugar, and stir until dissolved. Return the pan to the heat, bring to the boil and boil rapidly until setting point is reached. Pour into warmed jars, cover and label.

PEACH AND RASPBERRY JAM

Makes about 3.5 kg (7 lb)

1 kg (2 lb) ripe peaches (weight after stoning)
1 kg (2 lb) raspberries
150 ml (¼ pint) water
2 kg (4 lb) sugar

Skin, stone and chop the peaches into small pieces; crack a few stones to remove the kernels. Place the peaches, raspberries and water in a preserving pan and simmer gently until tender. Remove from the heat.

Add the sugar, and stir until dissolved, then a few peach kernels. Return to the heat, bring to the boil, and boil rapidly until setting point is reached. Pour into warmed jars, cover and label.

BLACKBERRY AND RHUBARB JAM

Makes about 5 kg (10 lb)

4 kg (8 lb) blackberries
1 litre (1½ pints) water
2 kg (4 lb) prepared rhubarb
sugar

Simmer the blackberries in the water until tender. Rub through a hair or nylon sieve. Cut the rhubarb into 2.5-cm (1-inch) pieces, place in a preserving pan with the sieved blackberry pulp, and simmer until tender. Remove from the heat.

To each 1 kg (2 lb) fruit pulp and 1 kg (2 lb) warmed sugar. Stir until the sugar is dissolved. Return to the heat, bring to the boil, and boil rapidly until setting point is reached. Pour into warmed jars, cover and label.

STRAWBERRY AND GOOSEBERRY JAM

Makes about 2.5 kg (5 lb)

*750 g (1½ lb) gooseberries or 500 g
(1 lb) gooseberries and 250 g
(8 oz) redcurrants
150 ml (¼ pint) water
750 g (1½ lb) strawberries
1.5 kg (3 lb) sugar*

Place the gooseberries (or gooseberries and redcurrants) in a preserving pan with the water, and cook gently until beginning to soften. Add the prepared strawberries and continue cooking gently until the fruit is soft. Remove from the heat. Test for pectin.

Add the sugar and stir until dissoved. Return to the heat, bring to the boil and boil rapidly until setting point is reached. Pour into warmed jars, cover and label.

GOOSEBERRY JAM

Makes about 5 kg (10 lb)

*2.2 kg (4½ lb) gooseberries
1 litre (1½ pints) water
3 kg (6 lb) sugar*

Wash, and top and tail the gooseberries. Place in a preserving pan with the water. Simmer gently until quite tender. Test for pectin. Remove from the heat.

Add the sugar and stir until dissolved. Return to the heat, bring to the boil and boil rapidly until setting point is reached. Pour into warmed jars, cover and label.

The degree of greenness of the jam will depend on the variety and maturity of the fruit, and the length of time of cooking with the sugar.

GOOSEBERRY AND ORANGE JAM

Makes about 2.5 kg (5 lb)

1.5 kg (3 lb) gooseberries
finely grated rind and juice of 2
  oranges
300 ml (½ pint) water
1.5 kg (3 lb) sugar

Wash and top and tail the gooseberries and place in a preserving pan. Add the orange rind and juice, together with the water. Simmer gently until the fruit is tender. Test for pectin. Remove from the heat. Add the sugar, and stir until dissolved. Return to the heat, bring to the boil and boil rapidly until setting point is reached. Pour into warmed jars, cover and label.

RHUBARB AND ORANGE JAM

Makes about 2.5 kg (5 lb)

6 sweet oranges
1 kg (2¼ lb) rhubarb, trimmed and
  finely sliced
sugar

Scrub the oranges in warm water. Pare the zest from the oranges with a potato peeler and cut into thin strips, or grate finely. Squeeze the juice from the fruit, allowing flesh to go with juice. Place both fruits and rind in a preserving pan and cook gently until tender.

Weigh the pulp and to each 1 kg (1 lb) fruit add 1 kg (1 lb) sugar. Stir until the sugar is dissolved. Return the pan to the heat, bring to the boil and boil rapidly until setting point is reached. Pour into warmed jars, cover and label.

RHUBARB AND GINGER JAM

Makes about 2.5 kg (5 lb)

1.5 kg (3 lb) rhubarb
1.5 kg (3 lb) sugar
130 ml (4 fl oz) lemon juice
25 g (1 oz) root ginger, bruised

Wipe the rhubarb and cut into chunks. Place in a bowl layered up with the sugar. Add the lemon juice and leave to stand overnight. Transfer to a preserving pan, and add the ginger tied in muslin. Bring to the boil and boil rapidly until setting point is reached. Remove the root ginger. Pour into warmed jars, cover and label.

RHUBARB AND ELDERFLOWER JAM

Makes about 5 kg (10 lb)

3 kg (6 lb) rhubarb
12–18 heads of elderflower
3 kg (6 lb) sugar
grated rind and juice of 2 lemons

Wipe the rhubarb and cut into 1-cm (½-inch) chunks. Place in a bowl, layering up with the sugar. Tie the elderflowers in a muslin bag and place in the middle of the rhubarb. Leave to stand for 24 hours.

Transfer the contents of the bowl to a preserving pan, bring to the boil, boil for 2–3 minutes, and return all to the bowl. Leave to stand for another 24 hours.

Remove the elderflowers. Add the grated rind and juice of the lemons to the jam and transfer to the preserving pan. Bring to the boil and boil rapidly until setting point is reached. Pour into warmed jars, cover and label.

This jam has rather a soft set.

RHUBARB AND ROSE PETAL JAM

Makes about 900 g (1¾ lb)

500 g (1 lb) rhubarb, trimmed
500 g (1 lb) sugar
juice of 1 lemon
2 handfuls of scented rose petals (red
  if possible)

Wipe the rhubarb, cut into small pieces and place in a bowl. Cover with the sugar, add the lemon juice, and leave to stand overnight.

Chop the rose petals and add to the rhubarb. Transfer all to a preserving pan, bring to the boil and boil until setting point is reached. Pour into warmed jars, cover and label.

50 g (2 oz) finely chopped angelica (fresh or crystallized) can be used as an alternative to rose petals.

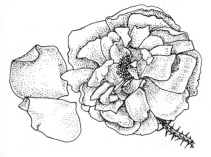

BLACKBERRY JAM

Makes about 5 kg (10 lb)

3 kg (6 lb) blackberries
150 ml (¼ pint) water
60 ml (4 tbsp) lemon juice or
* 300 ml (½ pint) apple pectin*
* stock or 1 level tsp citric or*
* tartaric acid*
3 kg (6 lb) sugar

Place the blackberries in a preserving pan with the water and the lemon juice or acid. Simmer until the fruit is cooked and reduced by about one-third. Remove from the heat.

Add the sugar, and pectin stock (if being used) and stir until sugar is dissolved. Return to the heat, bring to the boil and boil rapidly until setting point is reached. Pour into warmed jars, cover and label.

APPLE AND BLACKBERRY JAM

Makes about 2.5 kg (5 lb)

500 g (1 lb) blackberries
600 ml (1 pint) water
juice of 1 small lemon
1 kg (2 lb) cooking apples
1.5 kg (3 lb) sugar

Wash and drain the blackberries. Place in a pan with the water, and the lemon juice. Simmer gently until tender.

Peel, core and slice the apples and place in a pan. Strain the juice from the blackberries on to the apples and simmer until quite soft. Remove from the heat, add the sugar and stir until dissolved, then add the blackberries.

Return to the heat, bring to the boil and boil rapidly until setting point is reached. Pour into warmed jars, cover and label.

PUMPKIN/MARROW AND BLACKBERRY JAM

Makes about 3 kg (5½ lb)

2 kg (4 lb) pumpkin (or marrow)
1 kg (2 lb) blackberries
600 ml (1 pint) water
2 lemons
1.7 kg (3½ lb) sugar

Peel the pumpkin (or marrow) and remove the seeds. Cut into small neat dice and place in a preserving pan. Wash and stalk blackberries, add to the pumpkin, together with the water and grated rind of one lemon. Simmer gently until soft, then rub through a hair or nylon sieve.

Return to a clean pan, add the sugar and

stir until dissolved. Add the juice of the 2 lemons. Return the pan to the heat, bring to the boil, and boil rapidly until setting point is reached. Pour into warmed jars, cover and label.

APRICOT JAM (FRESH FRUIT)

Makes about 5 kg (10 lb)

3 kg (6 lb) fresh apricots
600 ml (1 pint) water
3 kg (6 lb) sugar

Wash the fruit, cut in halves and remove the stones. Crack a few stones, remove the kernels and blanch them by dipping in boiling water.

Place the fruit, kernels and water in a preserving pan, bring to simmering point, and simmer gently until the fruit is tender, and the contents of the pan reduced by one-third. Test for pectin.

Remove pan from the heat, add the sugar and stir until dissolved. Return pan to the heat, bring to the boil and boil rapidly until setting point is reached. Pour into warmed jars, cover and label.

APRICOT JAM (DRIED FRUIT)

Makes about 2.5 kg (5 lb)

500 g (1 lb) dried apricots
1.75 litres (3 pints) water
juice of 1 lemon
1.5 kg (3 lb) sugar
75 g (3 oz) blanched almonds

Wash the apricots and cut into small pieces, or chop coarsely in a food processor. Soak in the water for 12 hours. Place the fruit and water in a preserving pan, together with the lemon juice. Simmer until tender, about 30 minutes.

Remove from the heat, add the sugar and stir until dissolved, then add the almonds. Return to the heat, bring to the boil, and boil rapidly until setting point is reached. Pour into warmed jars, cover and label.

DRIED APRICOT AND GINGER JAM

Makes about 2.5 kg (5 lb)

500 kg (1 lb) dried apricots
1.75 litres (3 pints) water
125 g (4 oz) crystallized ginger
7 g (¼ oz) root ginger (bruised)
juice of 1 lemon
1.5 kg (3 lb) sugar

Wash the apricots and cut into small pieces or chop coarsely in a food processor. Soak in the water for 12 hours.

Place the apricots and soaking water in a preserving pan. Cut the ginger into small strips and add to the apricots, together with the bruised root ginger (tied in a muslin bag) and lemon juice. Simmer until tender, about 30–40 minutes.

Remove from the heat, add the sugar and stir until dissolved. Return to the heat, bring to the boil and boil rapidly until setting point is reached. Remove root ginger. Pour into warmed jars, cover and label.

AMBROSIA JAM

Makes about 3.1 kg (7¼ lb)

1 kg (2 lb) dried apricots
1 orange
2 lemons
Two 450-g (16-oz) cans crushed
*   pineapple*
sugar

Wash the apricots and cut into small pieces or chop coarsely in a food processor. Cover with cold water and leave to soak for 12 hours. After soaking, add the finely grated rind and juice of the orange and lemons, together with the contents of the cans of pineapple. Weigh the contents.

Place in a preserving pan, bring to simmering point, and simmer gently until the apricots are soft. Remove from the heat, add 1 kg (1 lb) sugar to each 1 kg (1 lb) fruit and juice (as weighed previously); stir until dissolved.

Return to the heat, bring to the boil and boil rapidly until setting point is reached. Pour into warmed jars, cover and label.

BANANA AND LEMON JAM

Makes about 900 g (1¾ lb)

500 g (1 lb) firm, ripe bananas, peeled
finely grated rind and juice of 3 lemons
500 g (1 lb) caster sugar

Peel and slice the bananas and place in a bowl. Add the grated rind and juice of the lemons, sprinkle the sugar over the fruit, cover the bowl with a plate and leave to stand until the sugar dissolves (about 1½ hours).

Transfer the contents of the bowl to a preserving pan, and simmer gently, stirring initially to ensure sugar is dissolved, until setting point is reached (about 15–20 minutes). Pour into warmed jars, cover and label.

BILBERRY JAM

Makes about 1.7 kg (3 lb)

1.5 kg (3½ lb) bilberries
150 ml (¼ pint) water
1 tsp tartaric or citric acid
1 kg (2 lb) sugar

Wash the fruit and place in a preserving pan with the water and acid. Simmer gently until the fruit is tender. Test for pectin. Remove from the heat.

Add the sugar and stir until dissolved. Return to the heat and bring to the boil, boil rapidly until setting point is reached. Pour into warmed jars, cover and label.

The set in this jam is never very firm.

GLENCAR JAM

Makes about 3.2 kg (7 lb)

500 g (1 lb) dried figs
2 kg (4 lb) rhubarb
finely grated rind and juice of 1 lemon
2 kg (4 lb) sugar

Chop the figs very finely and place in a large bowl with the finely sliced rhubarb and grated rind and juice of the lemon. Add the sugar, mix well. Allow to stand for 24 hours.

Transfer the mixture to a preserving pan, bring to the boil and boil rapidly until setting point is reached. Pour into warmed jars, cover and label.

PLUM JAM

Makes about 5 kg (10 lb)

3 kg (6 lb) plums
300–900 ml (½–1½ pints) water
3 kg (6 lb) sugar

Wash the fruit and place in a preserving pan with the water. Simmer gently until the fruit is tender, and the contents of the pan reduced by one-third. Test for pectin. Remove from the heat. Remove as many stones as possible as they rise to the surface.

Add the sugar and stir until dissolved. Return to the heat, bring to the boil and boil rapidly until setting point is reached. Pour into warmed jars. Cover and label.

PLUM AND ELDERBERRY JAM

Makes about 3.2 kg (7 lb)

1 kg (2 lb) elderberries
300 ml (½ pint) water
1.25 kg (2½ lb) plums
2 kg (4 lb) sugar

Remove the stalks from the elderberries and place in a saucepan with half the water. Simmer gently until tender; strain through a jelly bag. Stone the plums and cook in a preserving pan in the remaining water until tender. Add the elderberry juice; remove from the heat. Add the sugar, and stir until dissolved. Return the pan to the heat, bring to the boil, and boil rapidly until setting point is reached. Pour into warmed jars, cover and label.

DAMSON JAM

Makes about 5 kg (10 lb)

2.4 kg (4¾ lb) damsons
750 ml–1.25 litres (1¼–2 pints) water
3 kg (6 lb) sugar

Wash the fruit and place in a preserving pan with the water. Simmer gently until tender, and the contents of the pan are reduced by one-third. Remove as many stones as possible as they rise to the surface. Remove from the heat and test for pectin.

Add the sugar and stir until dissolved. Return to the heat, bring to the boil, and boil rapidly until setting point is reached.

BULLACE (OR DAMSON) AND PEAR JAM

Makes about 5 kg (10 lb)

1.5 kg (3 lb) prepared pears
1.5 kg (3 lb) bullaces or damsons
600 ml (1 pint) water
1 tsp citric acid
3 kg (6 lb) sugar

Peel and finely dice the pears. Remove the stones from bullaces or damsons. Place each fruit in a separate pan with 300 ml (½ pint) water in each, and add the citric acid with the pears. Simmer gently until both fruits are tender. Combine the two fruits in one pan and test for pectin. Add the sugar and stir until dissolved. Return to the heat, bring to the boil, and boil rapidly until setting point is reached. Pour into warmed jars, cover and label.

MILLIONAIRE'S MARROW JAM

Makes about 3 kg (6 lb)

2 kg (4 lb) prepared marrow
2 kg (4 lb) sugar
40 g (1½ oz) root ginger
finely grated rind and juice of 2
  lemons
25 g (1 oz) glacé cherries, finely
  chopped
small can pineapple pieces (optional)
1 tsp cayenne pepper
100 ml (4 fl oz) whisky

Peel the marrow, remove seeds and cut into small, neat dice. Place in a bowl and sprinkle with half the sugar. Leave overnight.

Next day, bruise the ginger and tie in a muslin bag. Transfer the marrow to a preserving pan and add the grated rind and juice of the lemons, the ginger, cherries, drained pineapple, cayenne pepper, whisky, muslin bag and the remaining sugar.

Heat gently, stirring until the sugar is dissolved, bring to the boil, and boil until setting point is reached. Remove the ginger. Pour into warmed jars, cover and label.

The jam should be dark brown and firm.

PEAR, APPLE AND QUINCE JAM

Makes about 5 kg (10 lb)

1 kg (2 lb) cooking apples
1 kg (2 lb) cooking pears
750 g (1½ lb) quinces
pared rind and juice of 1 lemon
1.4 litres (2½ pints) water
3 kg (6 lb) sugar

Peel and core the fruits, and cut into pieces. Retain the peel and cores and tie them in a muslin bag with lemon rind. Place the fruits and water in a preserving pan with the muslin bag and simmer until tender. Remove muslin bag and squeeze out the juice. Remove the pan from heat.

Add the sugar and stir until dissolved then add the lemon juice. Return the pan to the heat, bring to the boil and boil rapidly until setting point is reached. Pour into warmed jars, cover and label.

JAPONICA JAM

Makes about 4 kg (10 lb)

2 kg (4 lb) japonica quinces
4 litres (7 pints) water
1 heaped tsp ground cloves
sugar

Wash the fruit, cut into eighths and place in a preserving pan with the water. Simmer gently until tender. Sieve.

Weigh the pulp. To each 1 kg (1 lb) of pulp add 1 kg (1 lb) sugar. Stir until sugar is dissolved then add the ground cloves. Return to the heat, bring to the boil and boil rapidly until setting point is reached. Pour into warmed jars, cover and label.

BLACKCURRANT JAM

Makes about 5 kg (10 lb)

2 kg (4 lb) blackcurrants
1.75 litres (3 pints) water
3 kg (6 lb) sugar

Remove the stalks and wash the fruit. Place in a preserving pan with the water. Simmer gently until the fruit is quite tender, and the contents of the pan reduced by one-third. Test for pectin. Remove from the heat.

Add the sugar and stir until dissolved. Return to the heat, bring to the boil and boil rapidly until setting point is reached. Pour into warmed jars, cover and label.

TUTTI-FRUTTI JAM

Makes about 3 kg (6 lb)

500 g (1 lb) blackcurrants
water
500 g (1 lb) redcurrants
500 g (1 lb) strawberries
500 g (1 lb) raspberries
2 kg (4 lb) sugar

Prepare the fruits by hulling, strigging etc. Place the blackcurrants in a pan and add sufficient water to barely cover. Simmer gently until tender. Add all the other fruits, and continue to simmer gently until all the fruits are tender. Test for pectin. Remove from the heat.

Add the sugar and stir until dissolved. Return to the heat, bring to the boil and boil rapidly until setting point is reached. Pour into warmed jars, cover and label.

MULBERRY JAM

Makes about 3 kg (6 lb)

1.5 kg (3 lb) ripe mulberries
500 g (1 lb) apples
water
1.75 kg (3½ lb) sugar

Place the mulberries in a preserving pan, and allow to simmer in their own juices until tender. Peel, core and slice the apples, place in a small amount of water in another pan and cook until soft. Mix the two fruit pulps together in the preserving pan. Add the sugar and stir until dissolved. Return to the heat, bring to the boil and boil rapidly until setting point is reached. Pour into warmed jars, cover and label.

WHORTLEBERRY JAM

Makes about 1.5 kg (2½ lb)

1 kg (2 lb) whortleberries
juice of 1 lemon
750 g (1½ lb) sugar

Wash the fruit, and drain thoroughly. Place in a preserving pan, crush with a wooden spoon, add the lemon juice, and simmer gently until the fruit is tender. Remove from the heat.

Add the sugar and stir until dissolved. Return to the heat, bring to the boil and boil rapidly until setting point is reached. Pour into warmed jars, cover and label.

HIGH DUMPSIE DEARIE JAM

Makes about 4.5 kg (9 lb)

1 kg (2 lb) apples
1 kg (2 lb) pears
1 kg (2 lb) plums
300 ml (½ pint) water
finely grated rind of 2 lemons
7–15 g (¼–½ oz) dried root ginger
300 ml (½ pint) water
sugar

Wash the fruit. Peel, core and finely dice the apples and pears. Remove stones from the plums. Place the fruits in a preserving pan with the water and lemon rind. Bruise the ginger and tie in a muslin bag; add to the fruit. Simmer gently until the fruit is tender, then remove the ginger.

Measure the pulp and to each litre add 600 g sugar or to each pint add 12 oz sugar. Stir until the sugar is dissolved. Return to the heat, bring to the boil and boil rapidly until setting point is reached. Pour into warmed jars, cover and label.

MATRIMONY JAM

Makes about 2.5 kg (5 lb)

500 g (1 lb) cooking apples
500 g (1 lb) pears
500 g (1 lb) Victoria plums
150 ml (¼ pint) water
1 tsp citric acid
sugar

Prepare the fruit. Peel, core and dice the apples and pears and stone the plums. Place the fruits in a preserving pan with the water and citric acid. Simmer gently until quite tender.

Measure the pulp, and to each litre of pulp add 750 g sugar or to each pint of pulp add 1 lb sugar. Stir until the sugar is dissolved. Return to the heat, bring to the boil and boil rapidly until setting point is reached. Pour into warmed jars, cover and label.

STRAWBERRY JAM (1)

Makes about 5 kg (10 lb)

3.5 kg (7 lb) strawberries
juice of 2 lemons
3 kg (6 lb) sugar

Prepare the fruit, and place in a preserving pan with the lemon juice. Heat gently and stir constantly until the volume is reduced by about one-third. Add the sugar and stir until dissolved. Bring to the boil, and boil

rapidly until setting point is reached.

Remove any scum immediately, then let the jam cool until a skin forms on the surface. Stir gently, and pour the jam quickly into warmed jars, cover and label.

Lemon juice is not necessary with the more acid varieties of strawberries.

STRAWBERRY JAM (2)

Makes about 2.5 kg (5 lb)

225 g (8 oz) gooseberries or
*   redcurrants*
300 ml (½ pint) water
1.5 kg (3 lb) strawberries
1.5 kg (3 lb) sugar

Place the gooseberries or redcurrants in a pan with the water and cook gently until soft. Strain off the juice.

Place the prepared strawberries in a preserving pan, add the strained juice and cook gently, stirring constantly, until the fruit is soft. Remove from the heat.

Add the sugar and stir until dissolved. Return to the heat, bring to the boil and boil rapidly until setting point is reached. Remove any scum immediately. Allow the jam to cool slightly until a skin forms. Pour into warmed jars, cover and label.

RHUBARB AND RASPBERRY JAM

Makes about 3.5 kg (7 lb)

1.5 kg (3 lb) rhubarb, trimmed
2 kg (4 lb) sugar
1 kg (2 lb) raspberries

Wash the rhubarb and cut into small cubes. Place in layers with the sugar in a bowl. Leave overnight.

Transfer the contents of the bowl to a preserving pan and bring slowly to the boil. Add the lightly crushed raspberries and bring to the boil. Boil until setting point is reached. Pour into warmed jars. Cover and label.

SWISS JAM

Makes about 5 kg (10 lb)

500 g (1 lb) redcurrants
3 kg (6 lb) Morello cherries
200 ml (¼ pint) water
juice of 2 lemons
3 kg (6 lb) sugar

Place the redcurrants in a pan with the water and simmer gently until tender. Strain off the juice. Stone the cherries and place in a preserving pan; crack the stones and tie them in a muslin bag. Add to the pan together with the lemon juice and the strained redcurrant juice. Simmer gently until the cherries are soft. Remove the pan from the heat.

Add the sugar and stir until it is dissolved. Return the pan to the heat, bring to the boil, and boil rapidly until setting point is reached. Pour into warmed jars, cover and label.

MORELLO CHERRY AND REDCURRANT JAM

Makes about 2.5 kg (5 lb)

500 g (1 lb) Morello cherries
(weighed after stoning)
300 ml (½ pint) redcurrant juice
1.5 kg (3 lb) sugar

Wash the fruit, remove stones and place in a preserving pan with the redcurrant juice. Bruise the cherry stones, tie in a muslin bag, and add to the fruit. Simmer the fruit gently until tender. Test for pectin, remove from the heat. Remove the bag of stones.

Add the sugar and stir until dissolved. Return to the heat, bring to the boil and boil rapidly until setting point is reached. Pour into warmed jars, cover and label.

BLACKCURRANT AND RHUBARB JAM

Makes about 5.5 kg (11 lb)

2 kg (4 lb) blackcurrants
1.5 kg (3 lb) rhubarb
1 litre (1½ pints) water
3.5 kg (7 lb) sugar

Wash the fruit. Remove stalks from the blackcurrants and cut the rhubarb into 1-cm (½-inch) slices. Place the fruit and water in a preserving pan, bring to the boil and simmer gently until the fruit is quite soft (about 20 minutes). Test for pectin (see

pages 9–10). Remove from the heat.
Add the sugar and stir until dissolved.
Return to the heat, bring to the boil, and
boil rapidly until setting point is reached.
Pour into warmed jars, cover and label.

PLUM AND APPLE JAM

Makes about 3 kg (5 lb)

1.5 kg (3 lb) cooking apples
water
1.5 kg (3 lb) plums
sugar

Peel, core and slice the apples. Place in a
preserving pan with water to barely cover
and simmer until tender. Have and stone
the plums and add to the apples. Continue
cooking gently until the fruit is soft. Rub
through a hair or nylon sieve.

Measure the purée into a pan. To each
600 ml (1 pint) add 350 g (12 oz) sugar. Stir
until the sugar is dissolved. Return the pan
to the heat, bring to the boil, and boil
rapidly until setting point is reached. Pour
into warmed jars, cover and label.

GOOSEBERRY AND ELDERFLOWER JAM

Makes about 4.2 kg (8 lb)

2 kg (4 lb) firm green gooseberries
10–15 heads elderflowers
600 ml (1 pint) water
2.5 kg (5 lb) sugar

Wash and top and tail the gooseberries.
Place in a preserving pan with the water.
Gently rinse the elderflower heads, tie
loosely in a muslin bag, and place in the pan
with the gooseberries. Simmer gently until
tender. Test for pectin (see pages 9–10).
Remove from the heat. Squeeze the juice
from the muslin bag and discard it.

Add the sugar and stir until dissolved.
Return to the heat, bring to the boil and boil
rapidly until setting point is reached. Pour
into warmed jars, cover and label.

STRAWBERRY CONSERVE

Makes about 2.7 kg (6 lb)

2 kg (4 lb) hulled strawberries
2 kg (4 lb) sugar

Place the strawberries in layers with the sugar in a bowl and leave for 24 hours.
Transfer the contents of the bowl to a pan, bring to the boil and boil for 5 minutes. Return to the bowl and leave for 48 hours.
Again transfer the mixture to a preserving pan, bring to the boil and boil for 10–20 minutes until setting point is reached. Cool slightly until a skin forms. Stir gently. Pour into warmed jars, cover and label.

BLACK CHERRY CONSERVE

Makes about 1.25 kg (2½ lb)

1 kg (2 lb) stoned black or dark
cherries
1 kg (2 lb) sugar
300 ml (½ pint) redcurrant juice

Wash and stone the cherries. Dissolve the sugar in the redcurrant juice and bring to the boil. Add the cherries and boil for 10 minutes, stirring constantly. Drain the syrup from the cherries and return the syrup to the pan and boil hard until it begins to thicken.
Return the cherries to the syrup and boil again until setting point is reached. Remove any scum. Cool slightly until a skin forms. Stir gently and pour into warmed jars, cover and label.

PEAR AND GINGER CONSERVE

Makes about 2.5 kg (5 lb)

2 kg (4 lb) hard pears
1.5 kg (3 lb) sugar
50–100 g (2–4 oz) stem ginger
2 lemons

Peel, core and cut into quarters (eighths, if large) the pears and place in a bowl in layers with the sugar. Cover and leave to stand for 24 hours.
Chop the ginger and add to the pears with the grated rind and juice of the lemons.

Transfer all to a preserving pan and heat gently, stirring constantly, until all the sugar is dissolved. Bring to the boil and boil gently until the fruit is transparent and setting point is reached. Cool slightly before pouring into warmed jars. Cover and label.

PEAR AND GRAPE CONSERVE

Makes about 1.5 kg (3 lb)

750 g (1½ lb) black grapes
2.5-cm (1-inch) piece cinnamon stick
water
juice of 3 lemons
750 g (1½ lb) dessert pears
    (barely ripe)
sugar

Wash the grapes and place in a pan with the cinnamon stick and 4 tablespoons water. Simmer gently until soft. Sieve and make up to 600 ml (1 pint) with water, if necessary. Add the lemon juice and place in a preserving pan.

Peel and core the pears and slice thinly. Add to the grape purée and cook gently until tender and the pears appear transparent. Measure the pulp and to each 600 ml (1 pint) add 350 g (12 oz) sugar. Stir over a low heat until the sugar is dissolved. Bring to the boil and boil rapidly until setting point is reached. Pour into warmed jars, cover and label.

RHUBARB CONSERVE

Makes about 3.6 kg (8 lb)

2 kg (4 lb) rhubarb
500 g (1 lb) raisins, coarsely
    chopped
1.7 kg (3½ lb) sugar
2 oranges
1 lemon

Wipe the rhubarb and cut into 2.5-cm (1-inch) lengths. Place in a preserving pan with the sugar and raisins. Cook gently for 20 minutes. Add the juice of the oranges and lemon. Remove the white pith from the orange peel and shred the peel finely; add to the pan. Bring to the boil and boil gently until the syrup is thick and jelly-like. Pour into warmed jars, cover and label.

APRICOT AND ORANGE CONSERVE

Makes about 2.8 kg (6 lb)

500 g (1 lb) dried apricots
1.75 litres (3 pints) water
2 oranges
1.5 kg (3¼ lb) sugar
juice of 2 lemons
50 g (2 oz) walnuts, chopped

Wash the apricots and if large, cut up roughly. Place in a bowl and cover with the water. Scrub the oranges and remove the peel as for eating. Remove as much white pith as possible and slice the peel thinly. Chop the flesh coarsely. Place pith and pips in a muslin bag. Place all these with the apricots. Cover and leave to soak for 24 hours.

Transfer to a preserving pan, cover and simmer gently until soft. Remove muslin bag after squeezing out the juice. Remove from the heat, add the sugar and lemon juice, and stir until sugar is dissolved.

Return to the heat, bring to the boil and boil rapidly until setting point is reached. Stir in the chopped walnuts. Pour into warmed jars, cover and label.

APPLE AND PEAR CONSERVE

Makes about 3.8 kg (9 lb)

1.5 kg (3½ lb) cooking apples
1.5 kg (3½ lb) dessert pears
100 g (4 oz) chopped candied peel
grated rind and juice of 2 lemons
2.25 kg (5 lb) sugar

Peel and core the apples and pears, cut into neat small dice. Place in acidulated water to prevent browning.

Drain the prepared fruit and place in a preserving pan with the candied peel and the grated rind and juice of the lemons. Cover the pan and cook very gently for 20 minutes, until the fruit is softened. Remove the pan from the heat, cover with a clean cloth and leave to stand for 24 hours.

Next day, add the sugar, place over a gentle heat and stir to dissolve the sugar. Bring to the boil and boil rapidly until setting point is reached. Remove any scum and leave to cool slightly until a skin forms. Stir gently and pour into warmed jars, cover and label.

SPICED QUINCE CONSERVE

Makes about 1.7 kg (3½ lb)

about 450 g (1 lb) quinces
about 450 g (1 lb) oranges
1 lemon
1.25 kg (2½ lb) sugar
1 cinnamon stick
water

Peel and core the quinces and cut into small pieces. Place in a pan with sufficient water to cover, and cook gently until soft, adding more water if necessary to prevent burning. Rub through a sieve.

Place sieved pulp in a preserving pan together with the grated rinds and juice of the oranges and lemon. Add the sugar and cinnamon stick and stir until dissolved. Bring to the boil and boil rapidly until setting point is reached. Remove cinnamon stick. Pour into warmed jars, cover and label.

TOMATO AND APPLE CONSERVE

Makes about 1.5 kg (2¼ lb)

500 g (1 lb) ripe tomatoes
500 g (1 lb) apples
1 lemon
750 g (1½ lb) sugar
100 g (4 oz) cut mixed peel
100 g (4 oz) stem ginger, chopped

Skin and slice the tomatoes. Peel, core and slice the apples. Scrub the lemon, then mince it. Place all of these in a preserving pan and cook for 15 minutes.

Remove from the heat. Add the sugar and stir until dissolved. Return to the heat and simmer gently until the mixture thickens. Add the peel and ginger and stir well. Continue to simmer gently for a further 10 minutes. Pour into warmed jars, cover and label.

CHERRY CONSERVE

Makes about 1.4 kg (2½ lb)

1.2 kg (2½ lb) sugar
300 ml (½ pint) water
1 kg (2 lb) stoned cherries

Place the sugar and water in a pan and boil for 10 minutes. Add the prepared cherries, bring to the boil and boil for 25 minutes. Leave to stand for 24 hours.

Bring to the boil again and boil for 10 minutes. Pour into warmed jars, cover.

JELLIES

Jellies add variety to all meals, particularly as interesting accompaniments to many meats; for a change, when having roast pork, why not try sage jelly?

Jellies should be clear and sparkling. They are similar to jams in the principles of making, but as only the juice is used (all traces of pulp, skin, pips being removed) considerably more fruit is required than in jam making. Damaged and windfall fruit, providing it is underripe, can be used (the damaged parts being cut away). Economical and interesting jellies can be made by using fruits from hedgerows.

Jellies were traditionally potted in sloping sided jars, so that they could be turned out on to a plate for serving, but as these jars are virtually unobtainable nowadays, jellies are potted in small jars. not exceeding 450 g (1 lb) – the small jars aid setting. Jellies should be covered in the same way as jams.

It is misleading to give approximate yields for each jelly recipe as results depend on the type and quality of the fruit used and also on the growing season.

General Method
1. Fruits should be washed and any unsound parts removed. It is not necessary to stalk currants or peel apples, etc., but large fruits should be cut into smaller pieces.
2. Place prepared fruit in a large pan, adding sufficient water just to cover. (The quantity of water used depends on the kind of fruit – those with tough skins or hard fruits require longer cooking to soften, and therefore need more water).
3. Place the pan on the heat and simmer gently until the fruit is quite tender (about ¾–1 hour).
4. Pour into a scalded jelly bag and allow to drip (about 1 hour) until there is barely any liquid dripping from it. Do *not* squeeze the jelly bag. (Fruits rich in pectin can be extracted a second time – return the pulp to the pan with more water (half the original

amount used) and simmer again for 30 minutes –
pour into the jelly bag and allow to drip for a further
hour).

5. Test for pectin (see page 9).

6. Measure the strained juice into a preserving pan,
and bring to the boil.

7. To each 600 ml (1 pint) of juice add 450 g (1 lb)
sugar. Fruits rich in pectin will set 575 g (1¼ lb)
sugar to each 600 ml (1 pint).

8. Remove the pan from the heat, add sugar, and stir
until dissolved.

9. Return pan to the heat, bring to the boil and boil
rapidly until setting point is reached. Recommended
tests for setting point are the flake test and the temperature test (see pages 11–12).

10. Remove pan from the heat, remove any scum
immediately and pour into warmed jars. Gently
pouring the jelly into slightly tilted jars will help to
avoid air bubbles.

11. Cover the jars immediately as for jam (see page
11). Do not move the jars until the jelly has cooled.

BLACKBERRY JELLY

4 kg (8 lb) blackberries
juice of 3 large (4 small) lemons or
*   2 tsp citric or tartaric acid*
1 litre (1½ pints) water
sugar

Wash the fruit, place in a preserving pan
with the lemon juice or acid and water.
Simmer until tender.

Mash the fruit well and proceed from
stage 4 of the General Method (see page 35).

BLACKCURRANT JELLY

2 kg (4 lb) blackcurrants
1.85 litres (3 pints) water
sugar

Wash the fruit and place in a preserving pan with 1.25 litres (2 pints) water. Simmer until tender and mash well. Strain through a scalded jelly bag for 10–15 minutes.

Return the pulp to the pan, add another 600 ml (1 pint) water and simmer for a further 30 minutes. Then strain again.

Mix the two extracts together and proceed from stage 5 of the General Method (see above).

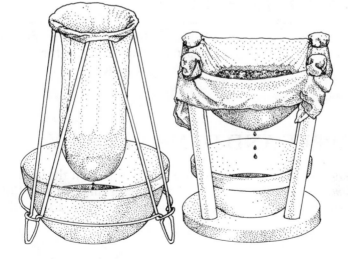

Jelly bag and stand, available from manufacturers of kitchen equipment

Several layers of scalded muslin tied to legs of a stool (as an alternative to jelly bag)

REDCURRANT JELLY

3 kg (6 lb) redcurrants
1.25–1.75 litres (2–3 pints) water
sugar

Prepare the fruit. Follow the method of making as for Blackcurrant Jelly (see page 37).

APPLE OR CRAB APPLE JELLY

apples
ginger or cloves
water
sugar

Choose apples with a definite flavour, or add flavourings such as ginger or cloves. Windfall apples can be used provided the damaged portions are cut out.

Wash and cut up the fruit and proceed as for the General Method (see pages 35–6).

If spices are used, these should be whole (not ground) and cooked with the apples.

APPLE AND SLOE JELLY

1.5 kg (3 lb) green apples
1.5 kg (3 lb) sloes
water
sugar

Rinse the fruit and cut the apples into quarters. Proceed as for the General Method (see pages 35–6).

CRAB APPLE AND DAMSON JELLY

3 kg (6 lb) crab apples
2 kg (4 lb) damsons
juice of 1 lemon
water
sugar

Rinse the fruit and cut the apples in halves. Place in a preserving pan with the lemon juice and water. Proceed as for the General Method (see pages 35–6).

RASPBERRY AND APPLE JELLY

*1 kg (2 lb) cooking apples
    (windfalls will do)
2 kg (4 lb) raspberries
water
sugar*

Cut up the apples and place in a large pan with the raspberries and sufficient water to barely cover. Simmer until the fruit is soft. Strain through a scalded jelly bag.

Proceed from stage 5 of the General Method (see page 36).

RASPBERRY JELLY

*4 kg (8 lb) raspberries
sugar*

Place the fruit in a large pan and heat gently until the juice runs, then mash well. Strain through a scalded jelly bag.

Measure the juice and add 450 g (1 lb) sugar to each 600 ml (1 pint) juice. Stir until dissolved. Return to the heat, bring to boil and boil rapidly until setting point is reached. Remove scum. Pour quickly into warmed jars, cover and label.

MINT JELLY (1)

*3 kg (6 lb) green apples
juice of 4 lemons or 2 tsp citric or
    tartaric acid
water
sugar
bunch of fresh young mint
green liquid food colouring
    (optional)*

Wash and cut the fruit roughly, place in a pan with lemon juice or acid and a few sprigs of the mint. Cover with water. Simmer to a soft pulp. Strain through a jelly bag. Test for pectin. Place the extract in a pan, bring to the boil. Add 500 g (1 lb) sugar to each 600 ml (1 pint); stir until it is dissolved. Boil rapidly for 5 minutes. Suspend the bunch of mint in the jelly and boil until setting point is reached. Remove mint, add colouring (if used). Remove any scum. Pour quickly into jars, cover and label.

MINT JELLY (2)

2.7 kg (6 lb) green apples
water
vinegar
sugar
fresh young mint
green food colouring

Wash and cut up the fruit. Place in a large pan with sufficient liquid to barely cover. To each 600 ml (1 pint) water add 150 ml (¼ pint) white vinegar.

Simmer gently to produce a soft pulp. Proceed as for Mint Jelly (1) (see page 39), but instead of suspending the bunch of mint in the boiling jelly, just before setting point is reached, add approximately 2 tablespoons finely chopped mint and a few drops of green colouring.

DAMSON JELLY

3 kg (6 lb) damsons
1.75 litres (3 pints) water
sugar

Prepare the fruit. Follow the method of making as for Blackcurrant Jelly (see page 37).

SAGE JELLY

1 kg (2 lb) crab apples or windfall
    apples
water
12 stems fresh sage
sugar
green liquid food colouring

Follow the method of making as for Mint Jelly (1) (see page 39). This jelly is excellent served with pork.

MULBERRY JELLY

3 kg (6 lb) mulberries
600 ml (1 pint) water
sugar

Follow the method of making as for the General Method (see pages 35–6).

LOGANBERRY JELLY

4 kg (8 lb) loganberries
water
sugar

Prepare the fruit. Follow the method of making as for Blackberry Jelly (see page 37).

LOGANBERRY AND REDCURRANT JELLY

1 kg (2 lb) loganberries
1 kg (2 lb) redcurrants
water
sugar

Prepare the fruit. Follow the method of making as for Blackberry Jelly (see page 37).

QUINCE JELLY

2 kg (4 lb) quinces
3.5 litres (6 pints) water
sugar
15 g (½ oz) citric or tartaric acid, if
    fruit is fully ripe

Wash the quinces, cut up finely and place in a large pan with 2 litres (4 pints) of the water. Cover and simmer until tender (about 1 hour). Strain through a scalded jelly bag. Return the pulp to a pan with the remaining water and make a second extract. Combine the two extracts and continue from stage 5 of the General Method (see page 36).

ROWAN JELLY

1 kg (2 lb) rowan berries
1 kg (2 lb) crab apples or windfall
    apples
water
sugar

Wash the berries thoroughly removing all leaves and twigs. Wash the apples and cut up roughly. Place both fruits in a preserving pan with sufficient water to barely cover. Simmer gently to produce a pulp. Strain through a scalded jelly bag.

Proceed from stage 5 of the General Method (see page 36).

GOOSEBERRY AND ELDERFLOWER JELLY

2 kg (4 lb) gooseberries
12 heads of elderflowers
1.25–1.75 litres (2–3 pints) water
sugar

Wash the gooseberries, but do not top and tail. Place in a preserving pan with water and proceed as for the General Method (see pages 35–6).

Tie the elderflower heads in a muslin bag. At stage 9, plunge the heads into the boiling jelly for a few minutes. This will be sufficient to impart a muscatel flavour to the jelly.

MEDLAR JELLY

2 kg (4 lb) medlars
2.5 litres (4 pints) water
sugar
lemon juice

Wash the fruit well, place in a preserving pan with the water and simmer slowly until fruit is soft and mushy. Pour into a scalded jelly bag and allow to drip for a few hours. Test for pectin (see pages 9–10).

Measure the strained juice into a preserving pan and add 1 tablespoon lemon juice to each 600 ml (1 pint) juice. Bring to the boil.

To each 600 ml (1 pint) juice add 350 g (12 oz) sugar. Stir until dissolved. Return to the heat, bring to the boil and boil rapidly until setting point is reached. Remove any scum. Pour quickly into warmed jars, cover and label.

ROSEHIP AND APPLE JELLY

600 ml (1 pint) fully ripe rosehips
1.5 kg (3 lb) green apples
water
juice of 1 lemon
sugar

Wash the rosehips thoroughly. Place in a pan and cover with water. Simmer gently until soft, then mash with a wooden spoon.

Wash the apples and cut up roughly. Place in a pan and barely cover with water. Simmer gently until soft. Strain the two

fruits together through a scalded jelly bag.
Proceed from stage 5 of the General
Method (see page 36) adding the strained
lemon juice with the sugar.

HIP AND HAW JELLY

1 kg (2 lb) rosehips
1 kg (2 lb) hawthorn berries
juice of 4 lemons
water

Proceed as for the General Method (see
pages 35–6), adding the strained lemon
juice at stage 6.

If haws are ripe before the hips, they can be
frozen until required.
As the berries absorb a lot of water whilst
softening, extra water may be required
during the cooking period.

RHUBARB AND ORANGE JELLY

1.5 kg (3 lb) rhubarb
1 kg (2 lb) oranges
2.5 litres (4 pints) water
sugar

Wash the fruits. Cut the rhubarb into
2.5-cm (1-inch) pieces; cut the oranges into
2.5-cm (1-inch) cubes. Place in a bowl with
the water and leave to soak overnight.
Transfer the contents of the bowl to a
large pan and simmer, covered, until the
peel is tender (1½-2 hours). Strain through
a scalded jelly bag.
Proceed from stage 5 of the General
Method (see page 36).

MARMALADES

It is difficult to find the origin of marmalade.
Nowadays a jam-like preserve made from citrus
fruits, where the peel is shredded, is called
marmalade. However, some other recipes use a
combination of citrus fruits and other fruits e.g.
apples and apricots. Some of these recipes have
been included.

The principles of making marmalade are essentially the same as those for making jam, with the exception that the peel of citrus fruits takes considerably longer to cook than the softer fruits used for jam, therefore more water is required for cooking.

Pectin. Much of the pectin necessary for a good set is found in the pith and pips of citrus fruits, and although in all finished marmalade, no pips are wanted and in some, the absence of pith and pips makes a far more appetising result, it is essential that the pith and pips are cooked to extract pectin.

Acid. As citrus fruits contain a much higher proportion of pectin than other fruits, extra acid must be added to obtain a good set. The quantity of acid to add is as follows: to 1.5 kg (3 lb) fruit add the juice of 2 lemons or 1 tsp citric acid or tartaric acid.

General Method
1. Scrub the fruit – dipping in boiling water for 1–2 minutes will help the skin to peel off.
2. Prepare the fruit according to the recipe. Simmer the fruit with the water and acid until the peel is tender (about 2 hours). Remove from the heat. Remove the bag containing the pips. Carry out the pectin test (see pages 9–10).
3. Add the sugar and stir until dissolved. Return to the heat, bring to the boil and boil until setting point is reached. (Tests for setting point – see page 11).
4. Remove from the heat and carefully skim off any scum. Allow to cool for 15–20 minutes until a skin forms. This cooling helps prevent the shreds from rising in the jar when potted. Gently stir in the skin. Pour into warmed jars and cover as for jams (see page 11). Label with type and date. Store in a cool, dry, dark, well-ventilated place.

GRAPEFRUIT MARMALADE

Makes about 5 kg (10 lb)

Either 1 kg (2¼ lb) grapefruit and
  350 g (12 oz) lemons
or 1.5 kg (3 lb) grapefruit and 2 tsp
  citric or tartaric acid
2.75–3.5 litres (4½–6 pints) water
3 kg (6 lb) sugar

Scrub and scald the fruit, then peel the fruit as for eating. Remove the pith from the skins and shred the peel finely. Place the shredded peel in a preserving pan with the acid if used and half the water. Simmer gently until the peel is tender, about 2 hours.

Coarsely chop the rest of the fruit and the pith and place with the remaining water in a pan. Cover and simmer gently for about 1½ hours. Strain through a colander, or rub through a sieve to make a thick marmalade. Add the strained pulp to the peel. Carry out a pectin test.

Add the sugar and stir until dissolved. Return to the heat, bring to the boil and boil rapidly until setting point is reached. Remove any scum. Allow to cool until a skin forms. Stir gently. Pour into warmed jars, cover and label.

SEVILLE ORANGE MARMALADE (1)

Makes about 5 kg (10 lb)

1.5 kg (3 lb) Seville oranges
2.75–3.5 litres (4½–6 pints) water
juice of 2 lemons or 1 tsp citric or
*   tartaric acid*
3 kg (6 lb) sugar

Either follow the method of making as for Grapefruit Marmalade (see page 46) noting that it is not necessary to remove any pith from the peel unless very thick.
or
Scrub the fruit, cut in half and squeeze out the juice. Tie the pips in a muslin bag. Slice the peel thinly, without removing the pith. Place in a preserving pan with the juice, the muslin bag and the water. Simmer gently until the peel is quite soft and the contents reduced by about one-third, about 2 hours.

Remove from the heat, squeeze the muslin bag to extract the juice then remove the bag. Test for pectin. Add the sugar and stir until dissolved. Return the pan to the heat, bring to the boil and boil rapidly until setting point is reached. Remove any scum, allow to cool slightly until a thin skin forms, then stir gently. Pour into warmed jars, cover and label.

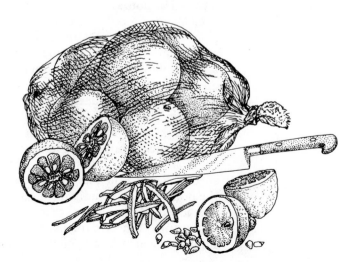

PUMPKIN MARMALADE

Makes about 3 kg (6 lb)

2 kg (4 lb) ripe pumpkin, peeled
3 Seville oranges
600 ml (1 pint) water
2 kg (4 lb) sugar

Cut the pumpkin in to small cubes, place in a bowl and cover with the sugar. Scrub the oranges, remove the peel and shred finely. Cut up the pulp roughly and tie the pips in a muslin bag. Place all these in another bowl and cover with the water. Leave both to stand for 24 hours.

Transfer the oranges to a pan and cook gently for about 1 hour until shreds are tender. Add the pumpkin and sugar, bring the mixture to the boil and boil gently until tender and setting point is reached. Remove any scum. Pour into warmed jars, cover and label.

JELLY MARMALADE

Makes about 2.25 kg (5 lb)

1 kg (2 lb) Seville oranges
2.75 litres (4½ pints) water
juice of 2 lemons
1.5 kg (3 lb) sugar

Scrub and scald the fruit, then peel the oranges as for eating. Remove the pith from the skins and shred the peel finely. Place the peel in a closed pan with 750 ml (1¼ pints) water and cook gently until quite tender (about 1½ hours).

Coarsely chop the rest of the fruit and place in another pan with the lemon juice and remaining water. Simmer gently for 2 hours. Drain the liquid from the shreds on to the pulp and strain through a scalded jelly bag. Do not squeeze. (A second extraction can be made as for jelly – see page 35). Carry out a pectin test.

Place the strained juice in a pan with the sugar and stir until dissolved. Add the shreds. Return the pan to the heat, bring to the boil and boil rapidly until setting point is reached. Remove any scum and allow to cool until a thin skin forms. Stir gently. Pour into warmed jars, cover and label.

SEVILLE ORANGE MARMALADE (2)

Makes about 2.5 kg (5 lb)

750 g (1½ lb) Seville oranges
juice of 1 lemon
1 litre (1½ pints) water
1.5 kg (3 lb) sugar

Prepare the fruit as for Seville Orange Marmalade (1) (see page 47). Place the prepared fruit and lemon juice in the pressure pan with the water. Put on the lid, leaving the vent open. Heat gently and when steam appears, close the vent and bring to 15 lb (H) pressure. Maintain pressure for 20 minutes, then allow pan to cool at room temperature for 10 minutes. Remove the bag of pips after extracting the juice. Test for pectin (see pages 9–10).

Add the sugar and stir until dissolved. Return the open pan to the heat, bring to the boil and boil rapidly until setting point is reached. Remove any scum. Allow to cool until a skin is formed. Stir gently. Pour into warmed jars, cover and label.

PINEAPPLE MARMALADE

Makes about 3 kg (6 lb)

1 lemon
3 large Jaffa oranges
525-g (1 lb 3-oz) can pineapple
1.5 litres (2½ pints) water
2 kg (4 lb) sugar

Scrub the lemon and oranges and peel as for eating. Cut the peel into small cubes. Coarsely chop the fruit, tying any pips in a muslin bag. Place all in a preserving pan, cover with the water and the strained pineapple juice. Simmer gently until the peel is tender. Squeeze the muslin bag to extract the juice, then remove the bag. Carry out a pectin test (see pages 9–10). Remove the pan from the heat.

Add the sugar and stir until dissolved then add the pineapple cut into small cubes. Return the pan to the heat, bring to the boil and boil rapidly until setting point is reached. Remove any scum. Allow to cool until a skin is formed. Stir gently. Pour into warmed jars, cover and label.

DARK THICK MARMALADE

Makes about 5 kg (10 lb)

1 kg (2 lb) Seville or bitter oranges
2 lemons
2.75–3.5 litres (4½–6 pints) water
3 kg (6 lb) sugar
25 g (1 oz) black treacle

Follow the method as for Seville Orange
Marmalade (1) (see page 47) but the lemons
should be sliced and included in the pulp.
Add the treacle with the sugar.

THREE FRUIT MARMALADE

Makes about 5 kg (10 lb)

2 grapefruit
4 lemons
2 sweet oranges
 total weight of fruit 1.5 kg (3 lb)
2.75–3.5 litres (4½–6 pints) water
3 kg (6 lb) sugar

Follow the method of making as for
Grapefruit Marmalade (see page 46).

LEMON AND WHISKY MARMALADE

Makes about 2.5 kg (5 lb)

750 g (1½ lb) lemons
1.5 litres (2½ pints) water
1.5 kg (3 lb) sugar
1 miniature bottle whisky

Scrub the lemons, cut in half and squeeze
out the juice. Place the pips in a muslin bag.
Slice the fruit finely and place in a
preserving pan with the juice, muslin bag
and the water. Simmer gently until tender
(about 2 hours). Squeeze the muslin bag to
extract the juice, then remove the bag. Test
for pectin. Remove from the heat.

Add the sugar and stir until dissolved.
Return to the heat. Bring to the boil and
boil rapidly until setting point is reached.
Stir in the whisky. Remove any scum.
Allow to cool slightly until a skin is formed.
Stir gently. Pour into warmed jars, cover
and label.

THICK LEMON AND GINGER MARMALADE

Makes about 5 kg (10 lb)

1.5 kg (3 lb) lemons
3 litres (5–6 pints) water
3 kg (6 lb) sugar
100–175 g (4–6 oz) stem ginger

Scrub the fruit, place in a covered pan with the water and simmer gently for about 1 hour, until the lemons are soft. Retaining the liquid in the pan, remove the lemons and cut the fruit in half. Remove the pips, tie these in a muslin bag and return to the pan. Slice the fruit and return it to the pan.

Return the uncovered pan to the heat and simmer gently for about 30 minutes, or until the original volume has been reduced by about one-third. Remove the pan from the heat and carry out a pectin test (see pages 9–10).

Add the sugar and stir until dissolved. Chop the ginger finely and add to the pan. Return the pan to the heat, bring to the boil and boil rapidly until setting point is reached. Remove any scum. Cool slightly until a skin is formed. Stir gently. Pour into warmed jars, cover and label.

LEMON OR LIME MARMALADE

Makes about 5 kg (10 lb)

1.5 kg (3 lb) lemons or limes
2.75–3.5 litres (4½–6 pints) water
3 kg (6 lb) sugar

Follow the method of making as for Grapefruit Marmalade (see page 46).

WINDFALL MARMALADE

Makes about 4 kg (8 lb)

2 grapefruit
4 lemons
1 kg (2 lb) windfall apples
    (weighed after preparation)
3 litres (5 pints) water
2.5 kg (5 lb) sugar

Scrub the citrus fruits, remove the zest from the fruit thinly using a potato peeler and then shred. Remove the pith from the fruit and chop the flesh roughly.

Roughly cut up the pith. Chop the prepared apples and place in a preserving pan with the prepared citrus fruits and the water. Tie the pith, pips and apple parings in a muslin bag and add to the pan. Simmer gently until the peel is tender and the quantity reduced by half. Squeeze the muslin bag to extract the juice then remove the bag. Carry out a pectin test. Remove from the heat.

Add the sugar and stir until dissolved. Return the pan to the heat, bring to the boil and boil rapidly until setting point is reached. Remove any scum. Allow to cool until a thin skin is formed, then stir gently. Pour into warmed jars, cover and label.

APRICOT MARMALADE

Makes about 4.5 kg (9 lb)

500 g (1 lb) dried apricots
750 g (1½ lb) Seville or sweet
    oranges
grated rind and juice of 1 lemon
1.8 litres (3 pints) water
3 kg (6 lb) sugar
25 g (1 oz) split almonds (optional)

Wash the apricots. Place in bowl and cover with 1.2 litres (2 pints) water, leave to soak for 24 hours. Transfer contents of the bowl to a preserving pan, add the grated rind and juice of the lemon and simmer gently until tender, stirring occasionally.

Meanwhile, scrub the oranges, cut in half and squeeze out the juice. Remove the pith from the peel and shred the peel finely. Place the peel and juice in a pressure cooker, together with the roughly chopped pith and pips tied in a muslin bag and 600 ml (1 pint) water. Bring slowly to 15 lb pressure (H) and cook for 20 minutes. Allow to cool 10 minutes before opening.

(Alternatively, cook in an open pan with at least 1.2 litres (2 pints) water for about 2 hours or until the peel is soft).

Squeeze the muslin bag to extract the juice, then remove the bag from the pan. Combine the two fruit pulps. Carry out a pectin test (see pages 9–10).

Add the sugar and stir until dissolved. Return to the heat, bring to the boil and boil until setting point is reached. Stir in the almonds. Pour into warmed jars, cover and label.

CARROT MARMALADE

Makes about 4.5 kg (9 lb)

500 g (1 lb) peeled carrots
500 g (1 lb) oranges
500 g (1 lb) lemons
3.5 litres (6 pints) water
3 kg (6 lb) sugar
1 tsp ground cinnamon

Finely chop the carrots and place in a preserving pan. Scrub the fruit, cut in half and squeeze out the juice. Remove the pith from the peel and shred the peel finely. Chop the pith roughly and place with the pips in a muslin bag. Place the finely shredded peel, juice and muslin bag in the pan with the carrots. Add the water and simmer gently for 1½–2 hours, until the peel is soft.

Squeeze the muslin bag to extract the juice and remove the bag. Remove from the heat and test for pectin (see pages 9–10).

Add the sugar and stir until dissolved, then stir in the cinnamon. Return the pan to the heat, bring to the boil and boil rapidly until setting point is reached. Remove scum. Allow to cool until a skin begins to form. Stir gently. Pour into warmed jars, cover and label.

BUTTERS, CHEESES AND CURDS

Butters and cheeses are an ideal way of using up an excess of fruit. Fruit cheeses are served in exactly the same way as dairy cheeses – cut into wedges. Curds are familiar in the lemon form, but in this chapter are some different combinations of fruits. Curds are not true preserves and should not be entered, when showing, in a class for 'any preserve'. Recipes for mincemeat and Cumberland rum butter are also included; again they are not true preserves.

Fruit butters and cheeses are made when there is a glut of fruit. Although they contain a large quantity of sugar, the proportion is less than that in jams.

Fruit butters are of a softer consistency than cheeses and are usually spiced and should be hermetically sealed. They are usually served as a spread.

Cheeses are cooked to a stiff consistency and set in small moulds so that they can be turned out for serving and cut into wedges.

Curds contain eggs and butter in addition to the fruit and sugar, and are not intended to keep. Strictly speaking they are not a true preserve. As the temperature reached during cooking is low, curds should only be covered with a wax circle and cellophane cover.

Unusual preserves, some of which are strictly speaking not preserves, all have their place on the larder shelf; they are also fun to make.

General Method
Wash the fruit, cut up if necessary, and place in a saucepan with sufficient water to barely cover. Simmer gently until soft. Sieve.

To make a cheese To each 500 g (1 lb) pulp add 500 g (1 lb) sugar. Stir until the sugar is dissolved. Boil gently for ¾–1 hour, stirring occasionally to prevent burning until a clean line is left when a spoon is drawn across. Pour into a mould which has been smeared with glycerine so that the cheese will turn out.

To make a butter To each 500 g (1 lb) pulp add 250–375 g (8–12 oz) sugar. Stir until the sugar is dissolved, add any spices and cook gently until a thick creamy consistency is reached. Pour into jars with airtight covers. Then process by immersing in a deep pan of hot water. Bring to the boil and boil for 5 minutes.

CUMBERLAND RUM BUTTER

450 g (1 lb) soft brown sugar
225 g (8 oz) butter
½ tsp ground nutmeg
2 tbsp rum

Ensure there are no lumps in the sugar by rolling between two sheets of greaseproof paper, or rubbing through a sieve. Place the sugar in a bowl.

Put the butter in a pan, heat gently until melted then heat until very hot but not disintegrating. Pour the butter on to the sugar, add the nutmeg, and stir until the butter is fully incorporated. Add the rum and stir again until well blended and a smooth texture.

Pour into an old-fashioned china bowl and allow to set.

APPLE BUTTER

3 kg (6 lb) crab apples or windfalls
1.25 litres (2 pints) water
1.25 litres (2 pints) cider
sugar
1 tsp ground cinnamon
1 tsp ground cloves

Wash the apples and chop roughly, removing any damaged parts. Place in a pan with the water and cider. Cook gently until soft. Sieve. Return the sieved pulp to the pan and simmer to obtain a thick consistency. To each 500 g (1 lb) pulp add 350 g (12 oz) sugar. Stir until the sugar is dissolved. Boil, stirring frequently until a thick creamy consistency is obtained. Pour into warmed jars, seal and process (see page 55).

MARROW ORANGE CREAM

Makes about 2.1 kg (3¾ lb)

1.5 kg (3 lb) prepared marrow
2 oranges
750 g (1½ lb) sugar

Peel and de-seed the marrow. Cut into large pieces and steam until tender (1–1½ hours depending on the age of the marrow). Leave to drain for several hours or overnight if possible to ensure that it is dry. Rub through a sieve or purée in a blender or food

135 g (4½ oz) butter
2 eggs (size 4)

processor. Place in a pan. Add the finely grated rind and juice of the oranges, together with the sugar and butter.

Cook over a low heat, stirring until the sugar has dissolved then simmer gently until the mixture thickens. Remove from the heat. Beat the eggs well, and strain on to the other ingredients. Mix well, return the pan to the heat and cook gently for 2–3 minutes. Pour into warmed jars, cover and label.

BRAMBLE CHEESE

1.5 kg (3 lb) blackberries
1.5 kg (3 lb) cooking apples
water
sugar

Wash the blackberries. Wipe the apples and chop up roughly. Place both in a pan with sufficient water to barely cover. Cover and cook gently until reduced to a pulp. Rub through a sieve. Return the sieved pulp to an open pan and cook further, if necessary, to reduce the pulp until thick. Weigh the pulp.

To each 500 g (1 lb) pulp add 500 g (1 lb) sugar and cook over a low heat to dissolve the sugar. Continue cooking until a thick consistency is obtained. When a spoon is drawn across the base of the pan, it should leave a clean line. Pour into prepared moulds. Cover as for jam (see page 11).

QUINCE CHEESE

quinces
water
sugar

Prepare quinces by washing and cutting into small pieces. Follow the method as for Bramble Cheese (see page 57).

DAMSON CHEESE

3 kg (6 lb) damsons
300 ml (½ pint) water
sugar

Follow the method for Bramble Cheese (see page 57).

PLUM AND APPLE CHEESE

1.5 kg (3 lb) cooking apples
500 g (1 lb) plums
water
sugar

Wash and cut up the apples without peeling. Wash the plums, and halve or quarter if large. Place both the fruits in a closed pan with sufficient water to barely cover.

Proceed as for Bramble Cheese (see page 57).

LEMON CURD (1)

Makes about 1.1 kg (2¼ lb)

4–5 lemons (225 ml/8 fl oz juice)
175 g (6 oz) butter
550 g (1¼ lb) sugar
4 eggs (225 ml/8 fl oz))

Wash the fruit and finely grate the rind from the lemons. Squeeze the juice and use 225 ml (8 fl oz). Place the butter, sugar, grated lemon rind and the juice in the top of a double saucepan, or in a bowl over a pan containing hot water. Cook gently until the sugar is dissolved. Strain and return to a clean pan or bowl.

Beat the eggs well, measure and strain on to the other ingredients. Return the pan to the heat and continue cooking over a low heat until the mixture thickens sufficiently to coat the back of a wooden spoon. Pour into warmed jars, cover and label.

APPLE LEMON CURD

Makes about 1.1 kg (2¼ lb)

450 g (1 lb) cooking apples
grated rind and juice of 2 lemons
4 tbsp water
450 g (1 lb) sugar
4 eggs (size 4)
125 g (4 oz) butter

Peel, core and roughly chop the apples. Cook in a closed pan with the grated lemon rind and the water until reduced to a pulp. Beat well to remove any lumps (or purée in a food processor).

Add the lemon juice and sugar and stir until the sugar is dissolved. Beat the eggs well and strain on to the apple pulp. Add the butter. Cook over a low heat, stirring occasionally, until a thick creamy consistency is obtained. Pour into warmed jars, cover and label.

GOLDEN CURD

Makes about 630 g (1½ lb)

50 g (2 oz) butter
2 oranges
1 lemon
225 g (8 oz) sugar
4 eggs (size 3)

Place the butter in the top of a double saucepan, or in a bowl standing over a pan containing hot water, to melt. Scrub the oranges and lemons and then finely grate the rinds. Cut the fruit in half and squeeze out the juice. Add the rinds, juice and sugar to the butter and stir until sugar dissolves.

Beat the eggs and strain on to the fruit mixture. Cook gently, stirring occasionally until the mixture thickens sufficiently to coat the back of the wooden spoon. Pour into warmed jars, cover and label.

LEMON CURD (2)

Makes about 300 g (10 oz)

150 g (5 oz) unsalted butter
225 g (8 oz) sugar
2 lemons
2 eggs

Follow the method as for Lemon Curd (1) (see page 58).

GOOSEBERRY CURD

Makes about 1.8 kg (4 lb)

1.5 g (3 lb) green gooseberries
600 ml (1 pint) water
750 g (1½ lb) sugar
750 g (4 oz) butter
4 eggs

Wash the gooseberries and place in a pan with the water. Simmer gently until tender then sieve. Place the sieved pulp in the top of a double saucepan, or in a bowl over a pan containing hot water, add the sugar and stir until dissolved.

Add the butter. Beat the eggs well and strain on to the other ingredients. Stir well. Cook gently, stirring occasionally, until the mixture thickens sufficiently to coat the back of a wooden spoon. Pour into warmed jars, cover and label.

ORANGE AND LEMON CURD

Makes about 500 g (1 lb)

150 g (5 oz) butter
225 g (8 oz) sugar
1 lemon
1 orange
2 eggs (size 4)

Follow the method as for Lemon Curd (1) (see page 58).

MARROW LEMON CREAM

Makes about 2.3 kg (6 lb)

2 kg (4 lb) prepared marrow
225 g (8 oz) butter
1.75 kg (3½ lb) sugar
6 lemons

Peel and de-seed the marrow. Cut into large pieces and steam until tender (1–1½ hours depending on age of marrow). Leave to drain for several hours, or overnight if possible, to ensure that it is completely dry. Mash into a smooth mixture or purée in a blender or food processor. Place in a pan with the butter, sugar and finely grated rind and juice of the lemons.

Cook over a low heat, stirring until the sugar has dissolved. Bring to the boil and

simmer, stirring occasionally, for
20–30 minutes. Pour into warmed jars,
cover and label.

PEAR HARLEQUIN

Makes about 2 kg (4 lb)

1.5 kg (3 lb) pears
450-g (1-lb) can pineapple pieces
grated rind and juice of 1 orange
sugar
150-ml (¼-pint) bottle maraschino
*   cherries*

Cut the pears into 1-cm (½-inch) cubes.
Add the pineapple pieces, and the grated
rind and juice of the orange. Weigh the
fruits and add three-quarters of their weight
in sugar. Sprinkle over the fruits and leave
overnight in a bowl.

Transfer the contents of the bowl to a pan
and simmer gently until thick. Meanwhile
cut the cherries in half and add to the fruit,
together with the maraschino syrup. Stir
well. Pour into wide-necked bottles
and seal.

This is excellent served with ice cream.

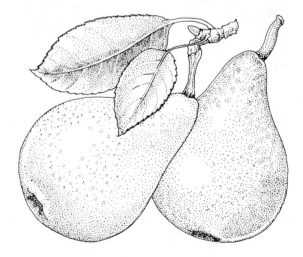

MINCEMEAT (1)

Makes about 3 kg (6 lb)

500 g (1 lb) cooking apples
  (prepared weight)
500 g (1 lb) currants
500 g (1 lb) seedless raisins
500 g (1 lb) sultanas
250 g (8 oz) chopped mixed peel
500 g (1 lb) suet, finely chopped or
  grated
500 g (1 lb) sugar (granulated or
  demerara)
grated rind and juice of 2 lemons
50 g (2 oz) almonds, blanched and
  shredded
½ tsp mixed spice (or to taste)
150 ml (¼ pint) whisky, rum or
  brandy (optional)

Mince the apples, currants, raisins and
sultanas coarsely. Mix all the ingredients
together (with the exception of the alcohol)
and leave covered with a clean cloth or cling
film at room temperature for three days,
stirring two or three times daily.

Stir in the alcohol (if used) and pack the
mincemeat into clean jars. Cover with a wax
disc and cellophane circle. Store in a cool
dry place.

A firm hard apple e.g. Wellington is
preferable to a Bramley seedling for good
keeping.

MINCEMEAT (2)

Makes about 800 g (1½ lb)

125 g (4 oz) Valencia raisins
125 g (4 oz) currants
125 g (4 oz) cooking apples, peeled
125 g (4 oz) demerara sugar
50 g (2 oz) sultanas
grated rind and juice of 1 lemon and
  1 orange
50 g (2 oz) suet, finely chopped or
  grated
40 g (1½ oz) chopped mixed peel
25 g (1 oz) blanched almonds,
  grated
1 tbsp brandy
1 tbsp rum
1 tsp mixed spice

Mince together all the fruits except the
currants. Add all the remaining ingredients
and stir well. Pack into clean jars and cover
with wax discs and cellophane circles. Store
in a cool dry place.

CRANBERRY AND ORANGE PRESERVE

Makes about 700 g (1½ lb)

225 g (8 oz) cranberries
1 medium orange
300 ml (½ pint) water
350 g (12 oz) sugar
50 g (2 oz) raisins
50 g (2 oz) walnuts, chopped

Wash the cranberries, finely chop the orange and place both in a pan with the water. Bring to boil and simmer for about 40 minutes. Add the sugar, the raisins and walnuts. Stir until the sugar is dissolved, return the pan to the heat, bring to the boil, and boil until setting point is reached (10–15 minutes).

Pour into warmed jars, cover and label.

The walnuts and raisins may be omitted to produce a variation.

AMERICAN PLUM GUMBO

1.5 kg (3 lb) plums
300–600 ml (½–1 pint) water
2 small oranges
1.5 kg (3 lb) sugar
500 g (1 lb) seedless raisins

Wash the plums, and if very large, halve or quarter. Place in pan with the water and simmer until a pulp is formed. Scrub the oranges, and slice thinly, removing the pips. Sieve the plums and place the sieved purée in a pan with all the other ingredients.

Cook over a low heat to dissolve the sugar. Continue cooking, stirring occasionally, until a thick pulp is obtained. Pour into warmed jars, cover and label.

VINEGAR PRESERVES

Here is a varied choice of pickles, some of the old favourites and also some interesting new ones. Flavoured vinegars are also included – fruit vinegars to help fight that tickling cough in winter and herb vinegars to give additional flavour to mayonnaise, and salad dressings.

Vinegar preserves allow for great individual scope. These preserves are mixtures of fruits and vegetables flavoured with spices, with sugar and vinegar acting as the preservatives. The vinegar used must be a good quality one containing not less than 5% acetic acid. Owing to the nature of vinegar great care must be taken in the choice of containers and covers. The cover must be one which will prevent vinegar from evaporating and yet also be unaffected by the acidity in the vinegar. The most suitable tops today are twist tops which have a plastic lining. Pliable plastic tops are available but these must be checked to ensure that they are a good fit on the jar. Porosan preserving skin is also suitable as it is vinegar-proof. Wax circles and cellophane tops are *not* suitable.

As vinegar preserves have such a variety of ingredients mixed together, it is necessary to keep them for a few weeks before using to ensure a good blend of flavours. It is recommended that pickles should be kept for six weeks before using, and chutneys for up to three months. There are a few, however, which can be used almost immediately but they will also improve further if allowed to mature.

The spices that can be used are many, and the personal choice of these adds greatly to the individuality of the finished preserve. Both whole and ground spices can be used, but if a clear, bright result is required, you must use whole spices tied in a muslin bag which can be removed before the preserve is potted. Whatever spices are used, remember that they should be fresh each year as their strength diminishes during storage.

Vinegars

Flavoured vinegars are often required in cookery, and it is very easy, and usually cheaper, to make these at home. Remember that top quality vinegar, containing 5% acetic acid, is required. Brown malt vinegar is usually used, but some light-coloured pickles require the use of white, or distilled, malt vinegar. Cider or wine vinegars can be used but their flavour is often masked by strong flavours in some pickles and they are expensive.

Spiced Vinegars
These can be purchased, but it is more fun to spice your own. Recommended quantities: to each 1 litre (2 pints) malt vinegar add 25 g (1 oz) mixed whole spices (cloves, cinnamon sticks, blade mace, allspice in equal amounts).

If a hotter flavoured vinegar is required a few peppercorns and 2–4 chillies may be added.

Cold Spiced Vinegar gives the best results (but needs plenty of forethought). Place the whole spices in the cold vinegar in the bottle and allow to steep for 4–8 weeks. Occasional shaking helps the full flavour to be extracted.

Hot Spiced Vinegar. Place vinegar and whole spices in a bowl covered with a plate, over a saucepan of cold water. Bring the water slowly to the boil, then remove the pan from the heat. Allow the spices to steep in the vinegar for 2 hours. Strain before use.

Herb vinegars
Half-fill a wide-necked jar with freshly gathered leaves, picked just before flowering. Fill to the top with white vinegar and allow to steep for at least 14 days before use. The herbs may be left longer if desired.

Fruit vinegars
Use equal quantities of fruit – usually soft fruit (e.g. blackberries, raspberries) and a good malt vinegar i.e. 500 g (1 lb) fruit to 600 ml (1 pint) vinegar.

Place in a bowl, cover and leave to steep for 3–5 days, stirring occasionally. Strain off the liquid, measure, and to each 600 ml (1 pint) add 500 g (1 lb) white sugar. Stir over a gentle heat until the sugar is dissolved, bring to the boil, and boil for 10 minutes. Put into bottles.

Pickles
There are two types: clear pickles, like pickled onions, and sweet pickles, like pickled damsons.

Clear pickles
It is necessary when making clear pickles to salt or brine the vegetables for 12–48 hours to extract some of the water from them. Block salt is preferable to vacuum-packed salt as it is less dense, but it is advisable to weigh salt to ensure that the vegetables are not oversalted.

For a cold brine use 500 g (1 lb) salt to 4.5 litres (1 gallon) water. The method is as follows:
1. Prepare the vegetables, cut into bite-sized pieces and place in a bowl. Cover with the brine, or alternatively sprinkle layers with salt. Cover the vegetables with a plate to ensure that they are under the liquid. Leave 12–48 hours in a cool place.
2. Rinse the vegetables carefully. Drain thoroughly.
3. Pack into jars and cover with spiced vinegar ensuring that there is at least 1 cm (½ inch) vinegar over the vegetables.
4. Cover the jars tightly with a vinegar-proof top (see page 65).

Sweet pickles
These are made from fruit and/or sweet vegetables. The fruit is stewed gently in sweetened, spiced vinegar until tender. Whole fruits need to be pricked before cooking to avoid shrivelling during storage.

PICKLED ONIONS

small onions
salt
water
spiced vinegar (see page 66)

Choose small, even-sized onions and place in a bowl. Make a brine using 500 g (1 lb) salt to 4.5 litres (1 gallon) water, pour over the onions and leave for 12 hours. Drain. Peel the onions and place in some freshly made brine and leave for 24 hours. They will float, so put a plate on top to keep them submerged. Drain and rinse thoroughly, removing surplus moisture. Pack into bottles and cover with cold spiced vinegar. Cover and label.

PICKLED RED CABBAGE

red cabbages
salt
spiced vinegar (see page 66)

Choose cabbages which are firm and a good red colour. Remove the core and slice finely. Place in a bowl, sprinkling salt between each layer. Leave to stand for 24 hours. Drain under cold running water and rinse well. Drain again, ensuring all surplus water is removed. Pack loosely into jars and cover with cold spiced vinegar. Cover securely and label.

This pickle is ready for eating in one week, and at its best if eaten before three months, after which it will lose its crispness.

MIXED PICKLE

A selection of:
    onions
    cauliflower
    cucumber
    marrow
    runner beans
brine
spiced vinegar (see page 66)

Prepare the vegetables and cut into bite-sized pieces, place in a bowl and cover with brine (see page 67). Leave to stand for 24–48 hours. Wash and drain very thoroughly. Pack neatly into jars and cover with cold spiced vinegar. Cover securely and label.

CUCUMBER PICKLE

Makes about 2.3 kg (5 lb)

3 kg (6 lb) sliced cucumber,
    unpeeled
250 g (8 oz) salt
2.5 litres (4 pints) water
1.8 litres (3 pints) white vinegar
1 tbsp celery seed
2 tbsp mustard seed
1½ tsp curry powder
1 kg (2 lb) sugar

Place the prepared cucumber in a bowl. Mix the salt and water, pour over the cucumber and leave for at least 6 hours, or preferably overnight. Rinse and drain thoroughly.

Place the remaining ingredients in a pan, heat gently until the sugar is dissolved, stirring frequently. Bring to the boil. Add the cucumber slices, return to the boil, and simmer gently for 4–5 minutes, stirring constantly. Pack into warmed jars, cover securely and label.

SHARP HOT PICCALILLI

Makes about 3 kg (6 lb)

3 kg (6 lb) prepared vegetables –
    diced cucumber, marrow, beans,
    small onions, cauliflower florets,
    green tomatoes (if liked)
500 g (1 lb) cooking salt
4.5 litres (1 gallon) water (optional)
15 g (½ oz) turmeric
25–40 g (1–1½ oz) dry mustard
25–40 g (1–1½ oz) ground ginger
150 g (6 oz) white sugar
1.2 litres (2 pints) white vinegar
20 g (¾ oz) cornflour or plain flour

Prepare the vegetables and brine or salt them as described on page 67. Rinse thoroughly under cold running water and drain. Mix the spices and the sugar in a large pan, and stir in most of the vinegar. Add the prepared vegetables and simmer gently until the desired texture is obtained – either crisp or tender. Do not cook until soft.

Blend the cornflour or flour with rest of the vinegar and add to the other ingredients. Bring back to the boil and, stirring carefully, boil for 2–3 minutes. Pack into warmed jars, cover securely and label.

BEETROOT PICKLE

Makes about 3.2 kg (7 lb)

1.5 kg (3 lb) boiled beetroot
750 g (1½ lb) cooking apples
  (prepared weight)
250 g (8 oz) onions, peeled
½ tsp ground ginger or 15 g (½ oz)
  mixed pickling spice
375 g (12 oz) brown sugar
750 ml (1 pint) vinegar
1 tsp salt

Prepare the beetroot by either dicing finely or mincing. Peel and core the apples and mince with the onions. If using pickling spice, tie in a muslin bag.

Place all the ingredients in a preserving pan, bring to the boil and simmer gently until the desired consistency is reached, stirring occasionally. Remove the bag of spices, pour into jars, cover and label.

PICKLED NASTURTIUM SEEDS

3 peppercorns
1 bay leaf
½ tsp salt
300 ml (½ pint) white vinegar
unripe nasturtium seeds

Place the spices and vinegar in a pan and simmer gently for 30 minutes. This vinegar may be prepared in advance and stored in a securely covered bottle.

Pick unripe nasturtium seeds on a fine day, wash and dry thoroughly. Place on greaseproof paper on a tray and leave in the sun for 3–5 days to dry thoroughly or place in a cool oven. Place in small jars and cover with the prepared vinegar. Cover the jars securely, label and leave for 2 months. Use as a substitute for capers.

SWEET PICKLED PRUNES

Makes about 1.5 kg (3 lb)

500 g (1 lb) dried prunes
1.25 litres (2 pints) sweetened spiced
  vinegar

Soak the prunes in water overnight.

Prepare the sweetened spiced vinegar as for pickled damsons (see page 71). Place the drained prunes in a pan with the vinegar and simmer until tender (take care not to break the prunes).

Remove the prunes from the vinegar and pack into jars. Boil the vinegar until

reduced to a syrup consistency, and pour
into the jars to cover the prunes. Cover
securely, label and store for at least 4 weeks
before eating.

PICKLED APRICOTS

1 kg (2 lb) sugar
600 ml (1 pint) white spiced vinegar
* (see page 66)*
1 kg (2 lb) fresh apricots

Dissolve the sugar in the vinegar. Prepare
the fruit by cutting in half, removing the
stones, and cooking in a little water until
just beginning to soften. Drain well.

Place in the sweetened spiced vinegar and
simmer gently for about ¾ hour, until just
tender – great care must be taken not to
overcook. Drain from the syrup and pack
neatly into jars.

Place the syrup back on the heat and boil
to reduce to a thick syrup. Pour over the
fruit in the jars. Cover and label.

PICKLED DAMSONS

4 kg (8 lb) damsons
rind of ½ lemon
2 kg (4 lb) sugar
15 g (½ oz) whole cloves
15 g (½ oz) whole allspice
15 g (½ oz) root ginger
15 g (½ oz) stick cinnamon
1.25 litres (2 pints) vinegar

Wash the damsons, prick thoroughly and
place in a bowl. Heat the rest of the
ingredients together gently in a pan until
the sugar is dissolved then pour over the
damsons. Leave to stand for 5–7 days.

Strain off the vinegar, place in a pan,
bring to the boil, pour over the damsons
and leave to stand for another 5–7 days.
Repeat once more.

Strain off the vinegar, place in a pan and
simmer gently to reduce to a thick syrup.
Meanwhile pack the damsons into jars.
Cover with the hot syrup. Cover jars
securely and label.

SWEET MILD PICCALILLI

Makes about 3 kg (6 lb)

*3 kg (6 lb) prepared vegetables –
  diced cucumber, marrow, beans,
  small onions, cauliflower florets,
  green tomatoes (optional)*
500 g (1 lb) cooking salt
4.5 litres (1 gallon) water (optional)
15 g (½ oz) turmeric
20 g (¾ oz) dry mustard
1½ tsp ground ginger
275 g (9 oz) white sugar
1.8 litres (3 pints) white vinegar
40 g (1½ oz) cornflour or plain flour

Prepare the vegetables and brine or salt them as described on page 67. Rinse thoroughly under cold running water and drain. Continue in the same way as for Sharp Hot Piccalilli (see page 69).

MILITARY PICKLE

Makes about 4 kg (8 lb)

1 marrow
1 cucumber
1 cauliflower
500 g (1 lb) runner beans
500 g (1 lb) onions
salt
7 chillies
15 g (½ oz) turmeric
15 g (½ oz) ground ginger
75–100 g (3–4 oz) plain flour
2.5 litres (4 pints) vinegar
500 g (1 lb) demerara sugar

Prepare the vegetables, and cut into bite-sized pieces. Place in a bowl, sprinkle with salt and leave overnight. Rinse in cold water and drain very thoroughly. Blend the spices and flour together with a little vinegar to form a smooth paste. Place the vegetables, vinegar and sugar in a pan, heat gently until the sugar is dissolved then bring to the boil and boil for 5 minutes. Add the blended spices, return to the boil, stirring constantly, and boil for 30 minutes. Pack into warmed jars, cover securely and label.

SPICED ORANGES

Makes about 700 g (1¾ lb)

6 oranges
water

Scrub the oranges and slice thickly. Place in a pan with sufficient water to cover. Bring to the boil and simmer gently until tender, about 1½–2 hours. Drain.

575 g (1¼ lb) white sugar
450 ml (¾ pint) white vinegar
1 tsp whole cloves
5-cm (2-inch) stick of cinnamon
1 tsp blade mace

Dissolve the sugar in the vinegar over a gentle heat and add the spices and lemon rind (tied in a muslin bag). Simmer for 10 minutes. Add the drained oranges, and simmer gently for about 1 hour.

Strain off the vinegar. Pack the oranges into warmed jars. Return the vinegar to the pan and boil rapidly to reduce to a syrup. Pour over the oranges. Cover securely, label and store.

SPICED CRAB APPLES

Makes about 1.5 kg (3 lb)

1.5 kg (3 lb) crab apples
500 ml (1 pint) vinegar
1 kg (2 lb) sugar
5-cm (2-inch) piece cinnamon stick
6 cloves
1 heaped tsp pickling spice

Place the vinegar and sugar in a pan with the spices (tied in a muslin bag). Heat gently to dissolve the sugar, stirring occasionally and then allow to simmer gently for 10 minutes.

Prepare the fruit by washing and de-stalking. Prick thoroughly, and if large, cut in half. Place in the sweetened vinegar and simmer gently until tender.

Strain off the vinegar, and pack the fruit into bottles. Return the vinegar to the pan and reduce to half by rapid boiling. Pour over the fruit. Cover the jars, label and store.

PICKLED BEETROOT

beetroots
water
salt
cold spiced vinegar (see page 66)

Choose small young beets, and prepare as for eating. Wash, place in a pan and cook in boiling salted water for 1–1½ hours. Cool, peel and slice. Pack the slices into bottles and cover with cold spiced vinegar. Cover and label.

CHUTNEYS

Chutneys add greatly to the choice of
accompaniments to serve with cold meats and
cheese. Spicy tomato chutney is superb with
cheese, and a homemade mango chutney is
excellent with curry.

A chutney is a vinegar preserve which offers great scope for individuality by the maker. It is a mixture of fruits, fresh and dried, vegetables, sugar, vinegar and spices, cooked slowly together to form a thick jam-like consistency. In a finished chutney, although some vegetables may retain a slightly crisp texture, there should be no 'free' vinegar floating at the top of the jar.

Care should be taken towards the end of cooking time to avoid the chutney burning on the base of the pan; occasional stirring and a low temperature help.

Chutneys should be poured into jars, filled to within 5 mm (¼ inch) of the top and covered as for other vinegar preserves (see page 65).

Vinegar has a slight hardening effect on some ingredients, especially onions and apples, so it is advisable to cook these ingredients in a little water to soften them before adding the rest of the ingredients.

Chutneys should be stored for two to three months before eating, although some of the present-day recipes which tend to be rather mild will be ready for eating almost at once. However, they lack character compared with the well-matured chutneys.

Chutneys after one year's storage

Covered only
with cellophane

Covered with a
metal twist-top

SPICY TOMATO CHUTNEY

Makes about 1.8 kg (4 lb)

500 g (1 lb) ripe tomatoes
500 g (1 lb) onions, peeled
500 g (1 lb) cooking apples
2 cloves garlic
1 large green pepper
300 ml (½ pint) vinegar
375 g (12 oz) brown sugar
1 tbsp salt
1 tbsp paprika
2 tsp prepared mustard
1 tsp chilli powder
1 tsp Worcestershire sauce
175 g (6 oz) tomato purée
¼–1 tsp cayenne pepper (to taste)

Dip the tomatoes in boiling water for ½–1 minute. Remove the skins and chop the flesh. Place in a saucepan. Chop or coarsely grate the onions; peel, core and slice the apples; crush the garlic and de-seed and chop the green pepper.

Add the onions, apples, garlic and peppers to the tomatoes with half the vinegar. Cover and simmer until the onions are soft. Add the remaining ingredients, bring to the boil and stir until the sugar is dissolved. Simmer uncovered until the desired consistency is reached. Pour into warmed jars, cover and label.

GREEN TOMATO CHUTNEY

Makes about 3 kg (7¼ lb)

2 kg (4 lb) green tomatoes
500 g (1 lb) apples
250 g (8 oz) stoned raisins
625 g (1¼ lb) shallots
15 g (½ oz) root ginger
8–10 chillies
2 tsp salt
500 g (1 lb) brown sugar
600 ml (1 pint) vinegar

Chop the tomatoes, peel and chop the apples and shallots and chop the raisins, or mince all the fruit. Bruise the ginger and tie in a muslin bag with the chillies.

Place all the ingredients in a preserving pan, bring to the boil, stirring until the sugar is dissolved, and simmer until the desired consistency is reached. Remove the muslin bag. Pour into warmed jars, cover and label.

RED AND GREEN PEPPER CHUTNEY

Makes about 3 kg (6 lb)

500 g (1 lb) red and green peppers,
    mixed
1 kg (2 lb) sour apples

Cut the peppers in half, and remove the stalks and seeds. Peel and core apples; peel the onions. Mince or finely chop the peppers, tomatoes, apples and onions. Place in a preserving pan.

750 g (1½ lb) onions
1 kg (2 lb) green tomatoes
25 g (1 oz) salt
40 g (1½ oz) bruised ginger,
    chillies, whole cloves, whole
    allspice, mustard seed and
    peppercorns, mixed
1 litre (1½ pints) vinegar
500 g (1 lb) sugar

Tie the spices in a muslin bag. Add to the pan with half the vinegar. Bring to the boil and simmer gently until thick. Add the remaining vinegar and the sugar, bring back to the boil, stirring until the sugar is dissolved and continue simmering until the desired consistency is reached. Remove the muslin bag. Pour into warmed jars, cover and label.

MANGO CHUTNEY

Makes about 2 kg (4 lb)

1 kg (2 lb) mangoes (fresh or
    canned)
750 g (1½ lb) cooking apples
125 g (4 oz) onions
125 g (4 oz) tamarinds
250 g (8 oz) stoned dates
125 g (4 oz) raisins
juice of 1 large lemon
500 ml (1 pint) vinegar
25 g (1 oz) salt
7 g (¼ oz) cayenne pepper
¼ tsp nutmeg
3 bay leaves
1½ tbsp lime juice
1 kg (2 lb) demerara or Barbados
    sugar

Peel and quarter the mangoes, if fresh. Peel, core and chop the apples. Peel and chop the onions. Stone and chop the tamarinds. Roughly chop the dates and raisins. Place all the ingredients except the lime juice and sugar in a large bowl, mix thoroughly and leave to stand for at least 3 hours.

Transfer to a preserving pan, bring to the boil and simmer gently until tender, stirring frequently. Add the sugar and lime juice, stir until the sugar is dissolved and continue to simmer until thick and of the desired consistency. Pour into warmed jars, cover and label.

RHUBARB CHUTNEY

Makes about 2.2 kg (4 lb)

1 kg (2 lb) rhubarb
2 lemons
25 g (1 oz) garlic
25 g (1 oz) root ginger
500 g (1 lb) sultanas
1 kg (2 lb) brown sugar
1 tsp curry powder
½ tsp cayenne pepper
600 ml (1 pint) vinegar

Slice the rhubarb finely and place in a preserving pan. Squeeze the juice from the lemons and strain on to the rhubarb. Crush the garlic and add to the pan. Bruise the ginger and tie in a muslin bag with the lemon skin.

Place the remainder of ingredients in the pan, and bring to the boil, stirring until the sugar is dissolved. Simmer gently until the desired consistency is reached. Remove the muslin bag. Pour into warmed jars, cover and label.

MARROW CHUTNEY

Makes about 1.5 kg (3 lb)

500 g (1 lb) marrow (prepared
  weight)
1 tbsp salt
500 g (1 lb) onions
500 g (1 lb) tomatoes
125 g (4 oz) sultanas
250 g (8 oz) sugar
3 chillies
3 cloves
1 pinch mixed spice
300 ml (½ pint) vinegar

Prepare the marrow and cut into small cubes, place in a bowl, sprinkle with the salt and leave for 24 hours. Drain.

Peel and chop the onions and tomatoes. Place all the ingredients in a preserving pan including the marrow and bring to the boil. Stir until the sugar is dissolved and then simmer gently until tender and the desired consistency is reached. Pour into warmed jars, cover and label.

PEAR, APPLE AND MARROW CHUTNEY

Makes about 3 kg (5½ lb)

1 kg (2 lb) marrow
75 g (3 oz) salt
1 kg (2 lb) cooking apples
1 kg (2 lb) cooking pears

Prepare the marrow and cut into small cubes, place in a bowl and sprinkle with the salt. Leave to stand for 24 hours. Drain. Place marrow in a steamer and cook until soft. Peel, core and slice the apples and pears and place in a covered pan with a little

125 g (4 oz) onions, chopped
1 tbsp plain flour
1 tbsp dry mustard
15 g (½ oz) cayenne pepper
25 g (1 oz) turmeric
25 g (1 oz) ground ginger
1.25 litre (2 pints) vinegar
500–700 g (1–1½ lb) sugar

water and the onions and cook gently until soft.

Mix the fruits and vegetables together, place in a preserving pan with the flour and spices and half the vinegar. Simmer gently until thick. Add the remaining vinegar and sugar, bring back to the boil, stirring until the sugar is dissolved and then continue simmering until the desired consistency is reached. Pour into warmed jars, cover and label.

PUMPKIN CHUTNEY

Makes about 1.8 kg (4 lb)

1 kg (1½ lb) pumpkin
600 ml (1 pint) vinegar
900 g (2 lb) sugar
225 g (8 oz) seedless raisins
125 g (4 oz) onion, chopped
25 g (1 oz) salt
tsp ground ginger
tsp pepper
¼ tsp ground nutmeg
juice of 1 lemon
½ tbsp grape juice
bay leaves

Prepare the pumpkin and chop into small dice. Place in a bowl with 300 ml (½ pint) vinegar and the other ingredients, mix well, cover and leave for 3 hours.

Transfer to a preserving pan, bring to the boil, stirring until the sugar is dissolved and then simmer gently for about 1 hour. Add the remaining vinegar and continue cooking until the desired consistency is reached. Pour into warmed jars, cover and label.

CUCUMBER AND APPLE CHUTNEY

Makes about 2.7 kg (5 lb)

1 kg (2 lb) cooking apples
675 g (1½ lb) onions
900 g (2 lb) cucumber
600 ml (1 pint) vinegar
450 g (1 lb) demerara sugar
15 g (½ oz) salt
½ tsp cayenne pepper

Peel, core and chop the apples. Peel and finely chop the onion. De-seed the cucumber. If ridge variety, peel as well. Chop finely. Place the apple, onion and cucumber in a pan with the vinegar, bring to the boil and simmer gently until soft.

Add the sugar, salt and cayenne. Heat gently, stirring until the sugar is dissolved, then continue simmering until the desired consistency is reached. Pour into warmed jars, cover and label.

APPLE CHUTNEY (1)

Makes about 4.5 kg (10 lb)

3.5 kg (7 lb) sour apples
30 g (1 oz) garlic
1.2 litres (2 pints) vinegar
250 g (8 oz) crystallized ginger
1.5 g (3 lb) brown sugar
500 g (1 lb) sultanas
1 tsp mixed spice
1 tsp cayenne pepper
1 tsp salt

Peel, core and slice the apples. Place in a pan with the finely chopped garlic and a small amount of water and cook, covered, until soft.

Add half the vinegar, the chopped ginger and all the other ingredients.

Bring to the boil, stirring until the sugar is dissolved then cook, uncovered, until beginning to thicken. Add the remaining vinegar and continue cooking until the desired consistency is reached. Pour into warmed jars, cover and label.

FRESH APRICOT CHUTNEY

Makes about 1.8 kg (3 lb)

250 g (8 oz) onions
750 g (1½ lb) apricots, prepared weight
1 clove garlic
2 tsp salt

Peel and mince the onions, place in a pan with a little water and cook, covered, until soft. Wash and de-stone the apricots and chop roughly. Crush the garlic in the salt. Crush the mustard seeds and tie with the allspice in a muslin bag.

Place all the ingredients in a large pan,

25 g (1 oz) mustard seed
½ tsp whole allspice
1 tsp turmeric
grated rind and juice of 1 orange
250 g (8 oz) sultanas
500 g (1 lb) demerara sugar
750 ml (1 pint) vinegar

bring to the boil, stir until the sugar is dissolved and then simmer gently until the desired consistency is reached. Remove the bag of spices. Pour into warmed jars, cover and label.

ORANGE CHUTNEY

Makes about 2.5 kg (5 lb)

500 g (1 lb) onions
1 kg (2 lb) cooking apples
2 kg (4 lb) sweet oranges
500 kg (1 lb) sultanas/seedless
  raisins
1 tbsp salt
2 tsp ground ginger
2 tsp cayenne pepper
2.5 litres (4 pints) vinegar
1 kg (2 lb) sugar

Peel and chop the onions, place in a covered pan with a little water and cook gently until tender. Peel, core and chop the apples and add to the pan. Continue cooking gently. Scrub the oranges and peel, removing as much white pith as possible. Mince the peel and pulp.

Place all the ingredients except the sugar with half the vinegar in a preserving pan and simmer gently until the orange peel is tender. Add the sugar and remaining vinegar, bring to the boil, stirring until the sugar is dissolved and continue simmering until the desired consistency is reached. Pour into warmed jars, cover and label.

LEMON CHUTNEY

Makes about 1.75 kg (3½ lb)

4 large lemons
450 g (1 lb) onions
25 g (1 oz) salt
600 ml (1 pint) vinegar
125 g (4 oz) raisins
15 g (½ oz) mustard seed, crushed
¼ tsp cayenne pepper
450 g (1 lb) demerara sugar
1 tsp ground ginger

Wash the lemons, cut into quarters, remove pips and slice finely. Peel and chop the onions. Place in a bowl, sprinkle with the salt and leave for 12–24 hours.

Place in a preserving pan with all the other ingredients. Bring to the boil, stirring until the sugar is dissolved and then simmer gently until tender and the desired consistency is reached. Pour into warmed jars, cover and label.

GOOSEBERRY CHUTNEY

Makes about 2 kg (4¼ lb)

1.5 kg (3 lb) gooseberries, topped
   and tailed
250 g (8 oz) onions, peeled
300 ml (½ pint) water
500 g (1 lb) sugar
15 g (½ oz) salt
1 tbsp ground ginger
½ tsp cayenne pepper
600 ml (1 pint) vinegar

Mince or finely chop the gooseberries and onions. Place in a covered pan with the water and cook until soft.

Add the rest of the ingredients, bring to the boil, stirring until the sugar is dissolved and continue cooking until the desired consistency is reached. Pour into warmed jars, cover and label.

BANANA CHUTNEY

Makes about 1.8 kg (4 lb)

450 g (1 lb) onions
125 g (4 oz) crystallized ginger
225 g (8 oz) stoned or block dates
8 ripe bananas (medium-sized)
15 g (½ oz) mixed pickling spice
2 tsp salt
300 ml (½ pint) vinegar
225 g (8 oz) black treacle

Peel the onions and mince together with the ginger and dates. Place in a preserving pan. Mash the bananas and add to the pan. Tie the pickling spices in a muslin bag and add to the pan together with the rest of the ingredients. Bring to the boil, stir until the sugar is dissolved and then simmer gently until the desired consistency is reached. Remove the bag of spices. Pour into warmed jars, cover and label.

PLUM CHUTNEY

Makes about 3 kg (6 lb)

1.5 kg (3 lb) plums
500 g (1 lb) onions
500 g (1 lb) apples
500 g (1 lb) sultanas
250 g (8 oz) sugar
25 g (1 oz) salt
1 tsp ground cinnamon
1 tsp ground allspice
1 tsp ground ginger
pinch cayenne pepper
1 litre (1½ pints) vinegar

Stone the plums and chop roughly. Peel and chop the onions. Peel, core and chop the apples and chop the sultanas. Place all the ingredients in a preserving pan, bring to the boil, stirring until the sugar is dissolved and then simmer gently until tender and the mixture has reached the desired consistency. Pour into warmed jars, cover and label.

MIXED FRUIT CHUTNEY

Makes about 3.5 kg (7 lb)

2 kg (4 lb) apples
500 g (1 lb) gooseberries and
    500 g (1 lb) green tomatoes or
    1 kg (2 lb) green tomatoes
500 g (1 lb) onions
1.5 litres (2 pints) vinegar
25 g (1 oz) pickling spice
250 g (8 oz) sultanas
750 g (1½ lb) brown sugar
25 g (1 oz) salt

Peel, core and chop the apples. Prepare the gooseberries and chop. Slice the tomatoes and peel and chop the onions. Place these ingredients in a preserving pan with half the vinegar and simmer gently until soft.

Tie the pickling spice in a muslin bag and add with the remaining ingredients to the fruit pulp and bring back to boil. Stir until the sugar is dissolved and then simmer gently until the desired consistency is reached. Remove the muslin bag. Pour into warmed jars, cover and label.

THREE FRUIT CHUTNEY

Makes about 2.3 kg (5 lb)

250 g (8 oz) dried apricots
1 kg (2 lb) marrow, prepared weight
20 g (¾ oz) salt
1 kg (2 lb) apples, prepared weight
15 g (½ oz) mustard seed
750 g (1½ lb) demerara sugar
75 g (3 oz) preserved ginger,
  chopped
1 tsp turmeric
2 tsp cornflour
½ tsp garlic, finely chopped
½ tsp cayenne pepper
1 litre (1½ pints) vinegar

Place the apricots in a bowl, cover with water and soak for 24 hours. Prepare the marrow, cut into small cubes, place in a bowl, sprinkle with the salt and leave to stand overnight. Drain well.

Drain the apricots and chop finely. Peel, core and chop the apples and place in a preserving pan with the apricots, marrow and a little water. Cover and simmer until a pulp is obtained. Tie the mustard seed in a muslin bag.

Add all the remaining ingredients and the muslin bag to the pan, bring to the boil, stirring until the sugar is dissolved, then continue to simmer, uncovered, until the desired consistency is reached. Remove the muslin bag. Pour into warmed jars, cover and label.

DAMSON CHUTNEY

Makes about 2.7 kg (6 lb)

2 kg (4 lb) damsons
750 g (1½ lb) apples
4 onions
750 g (1½ lb) raisins
3 cloves garlic
2 tbsp salt
2 litres (3 pints) vinegar
1 kg (2 lb) demerara sugar
25 g (1 oz) root ginger
25 g (1 oz) whole allspice
2 tsp whole cloves

Wash the damsons, place in a covered pan with a little water and cook until soft; remove the stones. Meanwhile, peel the apples and onions and either chop finely or mince. Mince the raisins. Crush the garlic with the salt. Bruise the ginger and tie in a muslin bag with the other spices.

Place all the ingredients in a preserving pan, bring to the boil, stirring until the sugar is dissolved, and then simmer gently until the desired consistency is reached. Pour into warmed jars, cover and label.

MARROW AND APPLE CHUTNEY

Makes about 3.5 kg (7 lb)

2 kg (4 lb) marrow
75 g (3 oz) salt
1 kg (2 lb) sour apples
500 g (1 lb) shallots
30 g (1 oz) bruised ginger, chillies
and peppercorns, mixed
500 g (1 lb) sugar
2 litres (3 pints) vinegar

Peel and cut the marrow into small pieces; layer up in a bowl with the salt between the layers. Leave for 12 hours, then drain.

Peel, core and chop the apples. Peel and chop the shallots. Tie the spices in a muslin bag. With the exception of the sugar and vinegar, place all the ingredients in a preserving pan. Bring to the boil and simmer gently until tender. Add the sugar and vinegar, stir until the sugar is dissolved and simmer until the desired consistency is reached. Remove the muslin bag. Pour into warmed jars, cover and label.

APPLE CHUTNEY (2)

Makes about 2.5 kg (5 lb)

1.5 kg (3 lb) sour apples
1 kg (2 lb) onions
500 g (1 lb) seedless raisins
750 g (1½ lb) brown sugar
finely grated rind and juice of
    2 lemons
2 tsp ground ginger
1 tbsp mustard seed
1 tsp salt
¼ tsp pepper
1.25 litres (2 pints) vinegar

Peel and core the apples. Peel the onions. Mince the apples, onions and raisins and place in a preserving pan. Add the grated lemon rind and strained juices and the rest of the ingredients.

Bring to the boil and simmer gently, stirring occasionally, until the desired consistency is reached. Pour into warmed jars, cover and label.

PEAR, DATE AND NUT CHUTNEY

Makes about 1.5 kg (3½ lb)

1.5 kg (3 lb) pears
125 g (4 oz) seedless raisins
125 g (4 oz) stoned dates
250 g (8 oz) walnut halves
350 ml (½ pint) wine vinegar
250 g (8 oz) brown sugar
juice of 3 lemons
2 tsp salt

Peel, core and chop the pears. Chop the raisins, dates and walnuts. Place all the ingredients in a preserving pan, bring to the boil, stirring until the sugar is dissolved, and then simmer gently until tender and the desired consistency is reached. Pour into warmed jars, cover and label.

BENGAL CHUTNEY

Makes about 2 kg (4 lb)

1 kg (2 lb) cooking apples, or green
   gooseberries
250 g (8 oz) onions
1 clove garlic
500 g (1 lb) raisins
500 g (1 lb) stoned dates
125 g (4 oz) preserved ginger
1 tbsp salt
¼ tsp cayenne pepper
1 litre (1½ pints) vinegar

Peel, core and chop the apples or top, tail and chop the gooseberries. Peel and slice the onions and garlic. Place these ingredients in a pan with a little water and cook, covered, until soft.

Mince the raisins and dates and chop the ginger. Place all the ingredients in a preserving pan, bring to the boil and stir until the sugar is dissolved. Simmer gently until the desired consistency is reached. Pour into warmed jars, cover and label.

APPLE AND APRICOT CHUTNEY

Makes about 3.1 kg (7 lb)

250 g (8 oz) dried apricots
2 kg (4 lb) cooking apples
500 g (1 lb) onions
500 g (1 lb) sultanas
500 g (1 lb) soft brown sugar
750 ml (1 pint) vinegar
1 tbsp salt
¼ tsp cayenne pepper

Place the apricots in a bowl with sufficient cold water to cover and leave to soak overnight. Peel, core and chop the apples. Peel and chop the onions. Drain and chop the apricots and sultanas.

Place all the ingredients in a preserving pan, bring to the boil, stirring until the sugar is dissolved, and then simmer gently until the desired consistency is reached. Pour into warmed jars, cover and label.

RIPE TOMATO CHUTNEY

Makes about 3.6 kg (8 lb)

6 kg (12 lb) ripe tomatoes
500 g (1 lb) onions, peeled
40 g (1½ oz) salt
2 tsp paprika
pinch of cayenne pepper
600 ml (1 pint) distilled spiced
    vinegar (see page 66)
750 g (1½ lb) sugar

Dip the tomatoes into boiling water for ½–1 minute, remove the skins and chop the flesh. Chop or mince the onions, place in a preserving pan with the tomatoes and cook until a thick pulp is obtained. Add the spices and half the vinegar and simmer until thick. Add the remaining vinegar and the sugar, bring back to the boil and stir until dissolved. Simmer again untitil the desired consistency is reached. Pour into warmed jars, cover and label.

APPLE CHUTNEY (3)

Makes about 3.6 kg (7 lb)

1.5 kg (3 lb) sour apples, prepared
    weight
500 g (1 lb) onions
500 g (1 lb) green tomatoes
250 g (8 oz) raisins
50 g (2 oz) crystallized ginger
1 litre (1½ pints) vinegar
500 g (1 lb) demerara sugar
25 g (1 oz) salt
½ tsp ground cloves
¼ tsp cayenne pepper

Peel and core the apples. Peel the onions. Finely chop (or coarsely mince) the apples, onions, tomatoes and raisins. Place in a preserving pan. Chop the crystallized ginger and add together with the remaining ingredients to the pan. Bring to the boil, stirring until the sugar is dissolved and then simmer gently until the desired consistency is reached. Pour into warmed jars, cover and label.

SAUCES AND RELISHES

As an accompaniment to any meal or as an extra ingredient in casseroles, homemade sauces are ideal. Relishes have arrived from the United States – they offer interesting textures and flavours and many may be eaten immediately.

Sauces

Sauces are made from similar ingredients to those in chutneys, but they are sieved part-way through cooking, to obtain a purée. If a good bright colour is required, as in a ripe tomato sauce, the sugar is not added until a short time before the end of cooking.

Sauces made from ingredients with a low acid content, such as ripe tomatoes, require to be sterilised after potting, to avoid fermentation.

Fill the bottles to within 2.5 cm (1 inch) of the top and screw the tops lightly into place. Place the bottles in a large deep pan with hot water reaching up to their necks, bring to the boil and allow to simmer for 30 minutes. After removing from the water, tighten up the tops, cool and label.

Relishes

Relishes are a mixture of fruit and/or vegetables with spices and vinegars. The method of preparation of relishes is such that the vegetables retain some of their crispness, through little or no cooking. Because the quantity of vinegar used is low, relishes *cannot* be considered as true preserves. They can be eaten immediately and most should not be kept longer than 6–8 weeks. They are a delightful accompaniment to salads and cold meats.

KEEPING MINT SAUCE

young mint, cleaned and chopped
vinegar
sugar
water

Fill a jar with mint. Cover with cold vinegar. Cover and store in a dark place. When required, remove the desired amount and place in a sauceboat. Add a little sugar; dilute with more vinegar and/or water. Sugar added to the stored sauce would cause fermentation.

RIPE TOMATO SAUCE

Makes about 3 litres (5 pints)

5-cm (2-inch) stick of cinnamon
7 g (¼ oz) whole allspice
7 g (¼ oz) blade mace
600 ml (1 pint) distilled or
*   white vinegar*
5.5 kg (12 lb) fully ripe tomatoes
40 g (1 ½ oz) salt
pinch of cayenne pepper
7 g (¼ oz) paprika
500 g (1 lb) sugar
3 tbsp tarragon or chilli vinegar

Tie the whole spices loosely in a muslin bag, place in a pan with the distilled vinegar and bring slowly to the boil. Remove from the heat, cover, and allow to infuse for 2 hours.

Wash and slice the tomatoes, place in a pan and cook until the skins are free. Rub the pulp through a sieve and return to a clean pan. Add the salt, cayenne pepper and paprika and cook until it begins to thicken. Add the sugar and flavoured vinegars and cook until a thick creamy consistency is obtained. Pour into warmed sauce bottles, cover and sterilise (see page 89).

MUSHROOM KETCHUP

Makes about 1.1 litres (2 pints)

1.8 kg (4 lb) mushrooms
100 g (4 oz) salt
1 ½ tsp allspice
1 ½ tsp black peppercorns
1 ½ tsp ginger
1 tsp cloves
1 tsp mustard seed
600 ml (1 pint) vinegar

Break the mushrooms into pieces, sprinkle with salt and leave to stand overnight. Rinse carefully. Mash with a wooden spoon. Place all the ingredients in a pan, cover, bring to the boil and cook for about 30 minutes. Strain into bottles and seal.

Sterilise, as described on page 89.

BLACKBERRY KETCHUP

blackberries
water
To each 600 ml (1 pint) pulp add:
½ tsp salt
125 g (4 oz) sugar
¼ tsp dry mustard
⅛ tsp ground cinnamon
⅛ tsp ground cloves
⅛ tsp ground nutmeg
300 ml (½ pint) vinegar

Place the blackberries in a pan with sufficient water to reach halfway up the fruit. Simmer until quite soft then sieve through a nylon sieve, and measure the pulp. Place the measured pulp in a saucepan with all the other ingredients and simmer for about 30 minutes or until the desired pouring consistency is reached. Pour into warmed bottles, cover and label.

GOOSEBERRY SAUCE

Makes about 1.3 litres (2 pints)

1.5 kg (3 lb) gooseberries
350 g (12 oz) onions
1 tsp ground ginger
1 tsp cayenne pepper
½ tsp salt
600 ml (1 pint) vinegar
500 g (1 lb) sugar

Wash the gooseberries. Peel and slice the onions. Place together in a pan with the spices, salt and half the vinegar, bring to the boil and cook until soft.

Sieve the pulp and return to a clean pan. Stir in the sugar and the rest of the vinegar. Cook gently until a creamy consistency is obtained, stirring occasionally. Pour into bottles, seal and label.

PLUM SAUCE

Makes about 2 litres (3½ pints)

4 kg (8 lb) plums
500 g (1 lb) onions
250 g (8 oz) currants
15 g (½ oz) root ginger, bruised
15 g (½ oz) whole allspice
7 g (¼ oz) chillies
7 g (¼ oz) peppercorns
7 g (¼ oz) mustard seed
1.2 litres (2 pints) vinegar
500 g (1 lb) sugar
50 g (2 oz) salt

Cut up the plums, peel and chop the onions. Place together in a pan with the currants, spices and 600 ml (1 pint) vinegar. Bring to the boil and simmer for 30 minutes.

Rub the pulp through a sieve and return to a clean pan. Add the sugar, salt and remaining vinegar, bring back to the boil, and simmer for 1 hour or until a creamy consistency is obtained. Pour into warmed bottles, seal and label.

WINTER RELISH

Makes about 3 kg (4½ lb)

500 g (1 lb) cooking apples
375 g (12 oz) onions
1.5 kg (3 lb) blackberries
500 ml (1 pint) vinegar
1 tsp ground cinnamon
1 tsp ground allspice
15 g (½ oz) ground ginger
2 tbsp salt
6 cloves
6 peppercorns
500 g (1 lb) white sugar

Peel, core and chop the apples. Peel and chop the onions. Place apples, onions and blackberries in a pan with the vinegar and spices, bring to the boil and simmer for 15–25 minutes.

Rub through a nylon sieve or a mouli-mill and return to a clean pan. Add the sugar, and stir until dissolved. Bring back to the boil and allow the mixture to boil rapidly until it thickens – about 20–30 minutes. Pour into warmed jars, cover and label.

TOMATO AND PINEAPPLE RELISH

Makes about 1.7 kg (3½ lb)

4 large cooking apples
525-g (1 lb 3-oz) can tomatoes
400-g (14-oz) can crushed pineapple
1.1 kg (2½ lb) sugar
½ tsp ground allspice
½ tsp ground cloves
½ tsp ground cinnamon
2 tsp Yorkshire relish (or brown sauce)
50 g (2 oz) salt
300 ml (½ pint) vinegar

Peel, core and chop the apples. Place all the ingredients in a saucepan and mix thoroughly. Bring to the boil and simmer gently until mixture thickens, stirring occasionally. Pour into warmed jars, cover and label.

CUCUMBER AND GREEN PEPPER RELISH

Makes about 1.1 kg (2¼ lb)

750 g (1½ lb) ridge cucumbers
250 g (8 oz) onion
1 green pepper
18 g (¾ oz) salt

Peel and dice the cucumbers, finely slice the onions and de-seed and shred the pepper. Place in a bowl with the salt. Leave to stand for 3 hours. Drain, rinse in cold water and drain again thoroughly.

Place the remaining ingredients in a pan,

300 ml (½ pint) white vinegar
150 g (5 oz) sugar
1 tsp turmeric
1 tsp mustard seed
1 tsp ground allspice
½ tsp ground mace

stir until the sugar is dissolved, then bring to the boil and simmer for 2 minutes. Add the drained vegetables, bring to the boil, and simmer for 4–5 minutes, stirring constantly. Pour into jars, cover securely and label.

This relish is ready to eat in a week.

CORN AND PEPPER RELISH

Makes about 1.75 kg (3½ lb)

750 g (1½ lb) sweetcorn kernels
2 large onions
2 red peppers
2 green peppers
2 tsp salt
2 tsp plain flour
1 tsp turmeric
2 tsp dry mustard
250 g (8 oz) white sugar
600 ml (1 pint) white vinegar

Place the sweetcorn in a pan containing 1 cm (½ inch) lightly salted, boiling water. Bring to the boil and boil for 3 minutes. Drain well. Peel and chop the onions. De-seed and chop the peppers.

Mix the salt, flour, turmeric, mustard and sugar together in a pan and blend in the vinegar. Add the sweetcorn, peppers and onions and stir well. Bring to the boil, and simmer gently for 30 minutes, stirring occasionally. Pour into jars, cover and label.

BEETROOT AND HORSERADISH RELISH

Makes 1.5 kg (3 lb)

500 g (1 lb) beetroot
250 g (8 oz) horseradish
pinch of salt
125 g (4 oz) sugar
300 ml (½ pint) white wine vinegar

Boil the beetroot until tender, peel and shred. Wash the horseradish and grate across the sticks to avoid getting long shreds.

Mix together the beetroot, horseradish, salt and sugar. Add the wine vinegar and mix thoroughly. Place in jars, cover and label.

This relish is ready for immediate use and will keep for about 4 weeks.

WHAT IS THE WI ?

If you have enjoyed this book, the chances are that you would enjoy belonging to the largest women's organisation in the country — the Women's Institutes.

We are friendly, go-ahead, like-minded women, who derive enormous satisfaction from all the movement has to offer. This list is long — you can make new friends, have fun and companionship, visit new places, develop new skills, take part in community services, fight local campaigns, become a WI market producer, and play an active role in an organisation which has a national voice.

The WI is the only women's organisation in the country which owns an adult education establishment. At Denman College, you can take a course in anything from car maintenance to paper sculpture, from book binding to yoga, or cordon bleu cookery to fly-fishing.

All you need to do to join is write to us here at the **National Federation of Women's Institutes, 39 Eccleston Street, London SW1W 9NT**, or telephone 01-730 7212, and we will put you in touch with WIs in your immediate locality. We hope to hear from you.

ABOUT THE AUTHOR

Pat Hesketh, a trained home economics teacher, has taught both cookery and crafts in schools, further education and adult education. Before joining the WI as Home Economics and Specialised Crafts Adviser in 1977, she was head of department of Rural Home Economics at the Staffordshire College of Agriculture.

As Adviser to the National Federation of Women's Institutes, Pat Hesketh has acted as consultant on several published craft and cookery books, and now travels extensively lecturing and tutoring WI members in all aspects of home economics and crafts.

INDEX